A Journey Through the Stilwell Road

A Journey Through the Stilwell Road

Edited by

Rakhee Bhattacharya
Binoda K. Mishra

Maulana Abul Kalam Azad Institute of Asian Studies, Kolkata

ANSHAH Anshah Publishing House

Views expressed here in various essays are those of the contributors and not necessarily that of the editors or institute.

ISBN: 978-81-8364-074-9

First Published in India in 2011

A Journey Through the Stilwell Road

Published by:

Anshah Publishing House

LG 18-19, Pankaj Central Market, Patparganj,
Delhi-110092, Tel: 91-11-2223 5152, 2223 6152
Br. Off. 4617/18, Ansari Road, Darya Ganj,
New Delhi-110002, Tel: 6594 6453, 9810522367

Acknowledgements

Maulana Abul Kalam Azad Institute of Asian Studies as a part of its Research Programme on North-East India organised a National Seminar on 'A Journey through the Stilwell Road,' at Kolkata on 23 September 2010. This volume has two parts; the first part consisted of a seminar, where scholars and policy makers expressed their views through presenting papers and through interactions about the idea of reopening the historic Stilwell Road in the broader framework of connectivity network of North-East India, Southwest China and Myanmar. The second part, more interestingly, was an exhibition of the photographs of the Stilwell Road. These photographs were taken during an expedition, which was undertaken by three eminent personalities, organised by MAKAIAS in the year 2009. The month-long expedition through this trail has brought out the actual scenario of the Stilwell Road and the concept of connectivity amongst the people through their cultural and merchandise activities among these three neighbours. Thus, their experience and various perspectives have become immensely important in the seminar and eventually in the volume.

The volume would not have seen the light of day without the persistent encouragement and support of Prof. H.S.

Vasudevan, the Director of Maulana Abul Kalam Azad Institute of Asian Studies. It is our privilege to work under his guidance and we extend our heartiest thanks to him. While organising this exhibition in a very short span of time, we worked as a team, and we are deeply thankful to our team-mates, Priyanka Basu, Abhik Samanta, Sanjay Pulipaka and Surajit De. Without their untiring support, we would not have made it a success. We are thankful to Dr. Reba Som, the Director of Rabindranath Tagore Centre, ICCR, Kolkata, for providing us the venue to organise the seminar and the photo exhibition. Our sincere thanks go to all the members of the administrative staff of MAKAIAS and our dear colleagues for their unfailing support. Last but not the least we are indebted to all the distinguished authors, whose contributions have given a shape to this book.

Rakhee Bhattacharya
Binoda K. Mishra

Contents

Acknowledgements v

1. Introduction 1
   Rakhee Bhattacharya

PART I

2. Stilwell Road: A Historical Retrospect 21
   D. Nath
3. The Lost Trail: The Stilwell Road in Historical and Contemporary Scenarios 45
   Lipi Ghosh
4. India-China Relations: No Need to Over Hype the Connectivity Factor 67
   D.S. Rajan
5. The North-East in India's Look East: A Focus on Connectivity and Development in the Region 79
   Soma Ghosal

6. Do We Need to Reopen the Stilwell Road? 101
Lt. Gen. J.R. Mukherjee (Retd.)

7. The Stillwell Road and India's Look East Policy 115
E.N. Rammohan

8. Connectivity and Economic Potential of Stilwell Road 123
Pradip Hazarika

PART II

9. Photo Essay on 'The Journey through the Stilwell Road' 140
Dilip Banerjee

Contributors 157
Index 158

1
Introduction

Rakhee Bhattacharya

The eternal human spirit of inquiry and adventure has always guided the movement of peoples across geographical barriers. The zeal for exploring beyond the discovered frontiers and an unquenchable thirst to know the unknown and to see the unseen, 'to strive, to seek, to find and not to yield' have been the driving forces behind the phenomenal progress of human civilization since times immemorial. To the unflinching human spirit, it is never 'too late to seek a newer world,......, to sail beyond the sunset, and the baths of all the western stars.'

Whether for survival, trade or merely for exploration, movement of peoples across vast distances spanning different countries and even continents has been integral to the spread of human civilization throughout the world. Since ancient times, people have been crossing the odds and barriers, travelling through uncharted routes into new lands and establishing connectivity with different countries, not always through peaceful means though.

The Indian subcontinent also has experienced numerous such movements of people, in the course exchanging ideas, education, culture, religion and trade; these have discovered new horizons and created new history. India has numerous overland routes, where wayfarers, travellers, traders, explorers, religious persona have crossed the borders, and charted out the trails that led to undiscovered territories. As rightly said by Majhi, 'in (the) course of long-drawn history, many a famous traveler, tourist and pilgrim came to India through hilly tracts, routes and passes. Their individual travelogues, and recorded accounts provide an interesting insight into the lifestyle and socio-economic conditions of the people belonging the relevant time. In a way they become instrumental in cementing social bonds and cultural unity, besides promoting two-way trade and commerce.'[1] But over a period of time, border areas of this country lost touch with the surrounding lands and their cultures, and many of them lost their trails and links due to shifts in priorities. Many cross-cultural and trans-border movements stopped due to the eventual closure of borders or due to various boundary disputes among these countries, at different times. One such lost trail, as mentioned by Ray was an alternative to the famous Silk Route of the 2nd century BC, when Chinese traders used to come to India by overland route from modern Yunnan through Upper Myanmar and Assam. This was usually the route for diplomatic missions between China and India and also those from Rome and Constantinople. This route greatly facilitated the large-scale cross country movement of people during that period in this region, but the trail eventually was lost around the 4th century AD for several hundred years.[2] Thus, the scholarly world claims that there existed a land route from Yunnan to Upper Assam passing through Bhamo, Kukwang and the Patkai Pass, which was believed to be a portion of the Southern Silk Road.[3] East and Southeast Asia always remained in close contact with India in terms of ethno-cultural and trade transactions and routes were created accordingly in terms of demands and priorities.

Around the 13th century, this overland route was rediscovered in a remote outpost of the earth called Ledo, in India's North-East, bordering Arunachal Pradesh on the North-Eastern boundary of Assam. Ahom documents like *buranji* and also the Shan chronicles of Burma provide elaborate information about this route, which was trailed by the Ahom king Siu-Ka-Pha from Mong Mao to reach and rule the Brahmaputra Valley, during 1228 AD. Phukan is of the opinion that Ahoms followed the Myitkyina-Patkai route from Waing Mao, as they came from the Chinese side, by the Mong Mao Route from Mong Mao.[4] The route today would pass through the territories of the present Arunachal Pradesh to reach Mytkina in Hukoong Valley in Myanmar, through the Pangsau Pass on the mighty Patkai range of mountains. This Ledo route was used for economic, cultural and political connectivity between the neighbouring nations of Burma, China and India's North-East. Over the centuries this meandering natural route was used for many hazardous journeys. Assamese chronicles, according to Nath, bear testimony to the use of this route in the past even by Buddhist and Hindu missionaries for visiting countries across the border and also by immigrant groups entering the Brahmaputra Valley from China and Myanmar. Tai Ahom is one such prominent migrant group, who had crossed the Patkai hills and entered the Brahmaputra Valley during the early part of the 13th century to rule Assam for long six centuries, till the beginning of the 19th century, when it was taken over by the British in the Treaty of Yandaboo (1826).[5] Donovan Webster, when he travelled through this route wrote:

- I crossed a stream culvert: its concrete is painted a humidity-stained brown; the creek beneath braids off through the vines. This road goes by many names – the Ledo Road, the Stilwell Road, Pick's Pike, the Man-a-Mile Road, the Uncle Sam Highway – but the most often it is called, simply, the Burma Road. And while historians may anoint it as one of the great engineering feats of World War II, the Old Soldiers have asserted – again and again – that it stands among the most forgotten routes in modern history. And more than anything, they believe it should remain that way.

- Just ahead, the road passes from India's state of Assam and into one called Arunachal Pradesh at the little border town of Jairanpur. After that, it turns back on itself and climbes between the two four-thousand-foot ridges of the Patkai Range, entering into

> Myanmar – the former Burma – at the second peak's summit on Pangsau Pass.[6]

The same route, which had been lying neglected for decades, gained fresh and renewed importance, and was rediscovered during World War II. The backdrop to this find was interesting. It was found to be the most useful for a counter-offensive against the Japanese, who created mayhem during World War II. In the words of J.N. Phukan, "The surprisingly quick advance of the Japanese army and their bombing of the towns and cities of Burma had caused a total disruption of communication; the British administration collapsed. As the Allied Army retreated, the strategic installations, oil refineries and bridges, including the famous Ava Bridge on the Irrawady, were blown up to check the Japanese advance. In the extreme panic, hundreds and thousands of non-Burmese, including Europeans, fled Burma for safety to India by whatever means of transport they could avail. The majority of them followed the land route from Myitkyina to Upper Assam that passed through Mogaung, Kamaing, Mainkhwan, Shinpyuin and Patkai Pass.'[7] This route was vaguely remembered by the British officials as the 'Old Opium Track', and was sometimes used by the local hill people, like Dshan, Singpho, Naga, for small trade and social visits. Thus, following the course of the 'Old Opium Track', a road was built on a high priority basis connecting the Upper Assam railhead town of Ledo with Myitkyina. Phukan is of the opinion that the whole length of the road was not newly constructed, as at several sectors good cart-roads already existed. Myitkyina was already connected by road with Bhamo, which was connected with Muse via Mansi. The total length of the route from Lekhapani in Assam to Muse on the China border, a distance of 820 km, was made suitable for heavy traffic. This road joins the Burma Road at Muse and then goes to the Chinese border to cross at Kinyang, 30 km, east from Muse. This newly built and improved road was renamed as Stilwell Road, after Joseph W. Stilwell, the U.S. General, who was appointed as the commander of the all-American forces in China, India, and Burma.[8]

The road that was now rebuilt by the American General Joseph W. Stilwell, was not for human movement but for a different purpose of carrying trucks loaded with coal to reach Kunming in China from Ledo, in January 1945. A part of this road stretching 61 kms today lies within Indian territory, while as much as 1,033 kms of it pass through Myanmar, and the rest 632 kms lie in China. However, during the post-War period, this meandering path which connected three close neighbours of this region again, got truncated due to changed geopolitical realities and perspective, and human contacts through this route also gradually reduced down to almost nothing. Thus, the Stilwell Road according to Deka became the proud moment of the past, but gradually over time the regained attraction as a potential passage for socio-economic development in the future generation, which connects three bordering countries. It also carries the history of World War II and tells the story of General Joseph W. Stilwell, the man behind the construction of the road. The road narrates the unforgettable story of at least 30,000 Indian, Chinese and Myanmar work forces without whose efforts, this road would not have come into existence.[9]

The international boundary of India's North-East since colonial times has remained closed due to several strategic and geopolitical sensitivities, and its economic and cultural links with these international neighbours simultaneously, has also got disrupted due to the closure of borders. But in recent times, North-East India has been relocated in the dynamics of development through an open door policy followed by India, and in this perspective the historical Stilwell Road, which connects India's North-East with China and Myanmar, also has gained renewed importance. A fresh thought is being given to the fact that this once-historical route has opened fresh opportunities. Not only will the lost links of the economy be re-established, but the lost bondage of emotions and culture and oneness that had come through the same route, will resurface. People of the region have a long-standing desire and hope of being able to connect themselves across the border and restore such lost links. The think tanks across various fora have started putting forward their views through various studies, policies, and seminars, highlighting the potentials of reopening this road. The present volume is one of such attempts, which has emerged as an interesting piece, having two distinct sections. The first section deals with a collection of eight essays, which have addressed the vector of issues that pivot around the reopening of the Stilwell Road. This collection of experiences and opinions by some prominent and veteran personalities and a group of young innovative scholars is intended to make this volume serve as useful inputs to our policy makers, scholars and thinkers and also members of the civil society.

The second part, which is the visual section, more interestingly, brings out the existing scenario of the Stilwell Road through several photographs. From Maulana Abul Kalam Azad Institute of Asian Studies, a three member team had undertaken a month-long expedition during April 2009, along this forgotten trail. This team consisted of a renowned photojournalist, Dilip Banerjee and two other scholars, Phalguni Motilal and Miss Niharika Gupta. The objective of this expedition was to know about this trail, which not only connects the geographical boundaries of three adjacent nations, but also, over centuries, actually has witnessed (though under different names for the same route) and provided space for cultural and economic exchange amongst the people of these three neighbours. So this idea of looking at the cultural affinities, economic interdependence and identifying the similarities in food habits and livelihood pattern that exist even today, despite the changing geopolitics and infrastructure pattern of this region, was primarily done by the team through first-hand information about the place by interacting and interviewing many unknown people while travelling, and by capturing innumerable images and pictures during their strenuous journey. As the team travelled around and made intense interactions with the people, they discovered tremendous emotional bondage and deep anthropological ties that still exist amongst the people of these three neighbouring countries. It was revealing to see that this border region of the Patkai range is inhabited by over a dozen ethnic communities. These groups are, as also mentioned by Barua, the Singphos (known as Kachin in Myanmar), Lisus, Tangsas, Noctes, Wanchos, Khamtis, Tai Phakes, Ahoms, Deoris and others. Thus territories bordering the Stilwell Road within the Indian side for example are inhabited by the people who are ethnically and culturally related to the people beyond the border. They have the same blood, culture, same clothing style, ornaments, food habits, language and scripts, and agricultural pattern.[10] This journey through the Stilwell Road therefore has remained fascinating to explore, experience and understand, as regards the emotional and also economic linkages which still exist amongst the people across the border. The photo essay in the book reveals such truths of life, a oneness that is hard to deny, but which over time has been painfully disconnected by man-made borders and barriers.

The essays in the first section have exclusively covered the time trend of the historical, current and future perspectives of this road. D. Nath, in his narration, extensively deals with the historical retrospect of Stilwell Road. While sketching about this road, the author has referred to the early historical evidence found in both India and China, which clearly highlights the land route connection across the Patkai range between North-East India, the Yunnan province of China and Upper Burma. He has referred to the visit of Hiuen Tsang in the 7th century A.D., to Assamese and Shan chronicles and to many more to justify the early existence of the route. Through such elaborate narration, the essay has brought out the importance of this route all through the ages. He mentions that 'as a passage of human migration this route has acted as the interweaving force between the countries of Asia in the past'. Thus the essay justifies that since India, Burma and China, are contiguous regions, therefore the strategic and political importance of this route needs to be realized.

In the next essay, Lipi Ghosh also has reiterated the historical perspective of this route and then has brought out the contemporary scenario. The author thinks that this route was historically a gateway to the outside world where merchants from home and from abroad used to do trade and thus had flourishing commerce and produced a great variety of commodities. Apart from this, the author says that the Tai-Ahom link also establishes the usage of this route. Then over the years the road gradually fell into disrepair, especially after Burma was liberated. And in course of time the Stilwell Road has virtually disappeared, since it lies in the lands of the three different nations of India, China and Myanmar, with 61 km in India, 632 km in China and 1,033 km in Myanmar. Following the Government of India's proposal, the author thinks that now reopening of this road as an international highway for trade to link Myanmar, China and other South East Asian countries will increase people's interaction and can improve neighbourhood relations. This can boost tourism and can develop the backward border lands and benefit the local people. The author proposes the creation of a Ledo-Bhamo-Dali Growth Triangle, which eventually can lead to overall economic development.

D.S. Rajan, while narrating on the broader perspective of India-China relations and connectivity issues, emphasizes a mutual understanding between the nations to carry forward the policies of engagement. The author thinks that the India-China congruence of interests has led to a substantial improvement in bilateral relations, which now have acquired a global character. On the connectivity issue, more specifically, Rajan points out that the boundary issue always comes first. Therefore talks at political levels, he feels, can bring some understanding between the nations in the spirit of 'mutual understanding and mutual accommodation'. China's military modernization also has become a cause of concern for India. China therefore needs to show a balance on its strategy of 'peaceful development goal' vis-à-vis its 'military modernization'. The author then suggests that both India and China can exploit the connectivity issue by addressing the issues that are non-strategic in nature; viz., river water dispute, trade imbalance, unskilled Chinese labour in India, and the importing of Chinese telecom equipment. Thus, efforts on the connectivity factor should continue, despite having strategic limitations, and he thinks the future leadership of these two nations also is important to resolve these issues.

Soma Ghosal in her essay has also pointed out the importance of connectivity and raised the issue of potential benefits for North-East India with the reopening of this historical route. The essay begins with the prospect of India's connectivity and economic growth with her eastern and south-eastern neighbours through the North-East region by emphasising Prime Minister Dr. Manmohan Singh's comment: "Look East Policy was not merely an external economic policy; it was also a strategic shift in India's vision of the world and India's place in the evolving global economy." And in November 2004, he referred to India's North-East as a gateway to an 'Asian Century' on the occasion of the flagging off of ASEAN – India car rally at Guwahati. The author points out that the Kunming Initiative of 1999, where BCIM members desired to facilitate trade amongst themselves and to develop regional resources, and reconstruction of the Burma Road, has remained one of the major projects under this initiative. From India's side, her Look East Policy has also heightened the trade relations and free market mechanism with its neighbours, which presupposes a solution to insurgency, poverty and economic backwardness, though the author here remains skeptic. She points out the remark of Mr. Pranab Mukherjee that though this policy hopes to be beneficial for India, at the same time it also becomes vulnerable by "opening up to South East Asia and flooding a fragile region with the logic of market economics." The author remains optimistic at the end and feels there lies ample scope for North-East India to prosper if the right steps are taken by the policy makers.

Lt. Gen. J.R. Mukherjee poses an interesting question in his essay by saying whether the Stilwell Road needs to be reopened as it fell into disrepair in the aftermath of Burmese liberation. It is assumed that with the reopening of this route, India's North-East, more specifically Assam and Arunachal Pradesh, would get the chance to be connected economically with flourishing parts of Yunnan and South East Asia via Myanmar. This would also facilitate India's Look East Policy. The road also can handle a substantial part of India's growing bilateral trade with China due to its cost and time benefits. Beyond this, the author also points out: "Stilwell Road has emerged (as) a serious contender as eastern India's entry point for the ambitious Asian Highway Network." Among the three nations, through which this road runs, China has already pursued the idea of reopening with diligence and has repaired and reconstructed its stretch of the road with a six-lane expressway. But on the contrary, Myanmar is still indecisive and has not engaged to renovate and reopen the road. While coming to the Indian side, it is still the security concerns of North-East India that predominate the issue along with heavy costs that is involved to reconstruct such mountainous terrain. The author therefore proposes several alternative routes along with the Stilwell Road to connect India's North-East with her important neighbours like China and Myanmar. Thus, the options suggested are reconstructing the Stilwell Road from Ledo in Assam to Myithina in Myanmar and linking up to the Chinese alignment to Kunming. Secondly, the other option suggested would be by extending the Indian road to Tamu from More, and further to Kalewa on the Chindwin River. By bridging the river, the author thinks it can link Mandalay, which is on the railway system of Myanmar with linkages onto the new road to Kunming. Thirdly, India's Mizoram can be connected to the Myanmar port of Sitwe and can provide access to the Bay of Bengal and also to Kunming – the Sitwe Corridor. The author has not ruled out the options of the Tripura-Bangladesh link through Chittagong port and utilizing the National Highway from upper Assam to the Chinese border at Kahao/Dichu. These routes have great developmental significance, provided security measures are taken in the right proportions.

E.N. Rammohan in his short essay made a very sharp observation on how China has become the predominant country in this region. He mentions that during 1989, the Burmese military sent the delegation to India for seeking help to build their armed forces and returned disheartened and then approached China. China immediately welcomed the delegation and helped then by supplying the needful. China at the same time had developed the part of the Stilwell Road that connects Kunming area with Lashio and then to Mandalay. This had given the Chinese a golden opportunity to create a huge market in Burma and soon Chinese goods and people had started flowing into Myanmar. Today China accounts as a very important trade partner for Myanmar, which supplies ready materials and imports raw materials from Myanmar. Ruili, the small border town of China has become the corridor for such flourishing trade. The author therefore feels that the time has come to reopen this entire Stilwell Road, so that legal trade gets a boost in this whole region and India can be a gainful partner in this business.

Pradip Hazarika in his essay also has echoed that the road needs to be immediately opened for purposes of connectivity, economic potential, trade opportunities, tourism potential and for making India's Look East Policy a success through integration. This reopening he feels can make different sub-regional plans become operational and India's engagement with various such regional co-operation can be a success. This, he thinks, can also improve people-to-people contact across the border.

All these essays by and large dwell upon the possibilities of reopening of the Stilwell Road, so that a win-win situation can be achieved in terms of economic and trade relations among the three neighbouring regions; India's North-East, China's south-west and Myanmar's north, which is likely to usher in prosperity for the people across the region through their untapped potentials like horticulture, floriculture, biodiversity and tourism. Through restoring connectivity, this stretch of land possibly can attempt to restore and remove the age-old asymmetry of development and economic opportunities. This lost trail can also regenerate the lost links of culture and contacts amongst the people, so that the region can again become a mingling place for people, products and ideas with free space for movements and interactions. Such connectivity is extremely important for modern regional integration. In the words of Hussain: "Stilwell Road underscores the importance of North-East India as the possible centre of economic resurgence. Reopening of the Stilwell Road will go a long way in opening up trans-border trade and solving insurgency problems of the North-East, though there is little doubt that it will need serious concerted efforts by all concerned. Reopening of this route will revive the close cultural, emotional and spiritual ties of a large number of ethnic groups living in the North-East of India, Myanmar and south-western China triggering a new era of travel, trade, tourism, pilgrimage and of course peace."[11] It is therefore time for these three nations to engage with each other and come to a consensus for establishing connectivity across the entire region. 'No man is an island entirely of itself' and this can improve the level of understanding as well as physical development by bringing people together, besides reducing security threats faced by us. But as pointed out by Sinha, of the three nations through which the Stilwell Road runs, it is Myanmar which needs more open collaboration to link Ledo with Kunming by road. China of course has energetically undertaken the repair and reconstruction of its stretch of the road and India's enthusiasm needs to be transformed into action.[12] If in future this historic road reopens and is remade, many of the unfulfilled dreams and hopes of the people of the present generation of the border areas may be translated into reality. As Lu Xun, the great Chinese author wrote once, "Hope cannot be said to exist, nor can it be said not to exist. It is just like roads across the earth. For actually the earth has no roads to begin with.... but when many people pass one way, a road is made."[13]

Notes

1. Prithibi Majhi 'Address of the Chief Guest', in D. Nath (ed), '*Reopening of the Stilwell Road: Prospects and Problems*', New Delhi, Anamika Publishers and Distributors (P) Ltd., 2004, p. 21.
2. A.K. Ray, the keynote address in D. Nath '*Reopening of the Stilwell Road: Prospects and Problems*' (ed), New Delhi, Anamika Publishers and Distributors (P) Ltd., 2004, p. 30.
3. J.N. Phukan, 'Stilwell Roadin Historical Perspective', in D. Nath '*Reopening of the Stilwell Road: Prospects and Problems*' (ed), New Delhi, Anamika Publishers and Distributors (P) Ltd., 2004, p. 43.
4. J.N. Phukan, 'Stilwell Roadin Historical Perspective', in D. Nath "*Reopening of the Stilwell Road: Prospects and Problems*" (ed), New Delhi, Anamika Publishers and Distributors (P) Ltd., 2004, p. 45.
5. D. Nath, "*Reopening of the Stilwell Road: Prospects and Problems*" (ed), New Delhi, Anamika Publishers and Distributors (P) Ltd., 2004, p. 1.
6. Donovan Wesbster '*The Burma Road: The Epic Story of One of World War II's Most Remarkable Endeavours*', Pan Books, 2003, p. 6.
7. J.N. Phukan 'Stilwell Roadin Historical Perspective', in D. Nath "*Reopening of the Stilwell Road: Prospects and Problems*" (ed), New Delhi, Anamika Publishers and Distributors (P) Ltd., 2004, pp. 37-39.
8. Ibid., p. 39.
9. Rani Mudiar Deka 'Reopening of the Stilwell Road: Prospects of Tourism Development', in D. Nath "*Reopening of the Stilwell Road: Prospects and Problems*" (ed), New Delhi, Anamika Publishers and Distributors (P) Ltd., 2004, p. 141.
10. S.N. Barua 'Restoration of the Stilwell Road: The Socio-Cultural Implications', in D. Nath "*Reopening of the Stilwell Road: Prospects*

and Problems" (ed), New Delhi, Anamika Publishers and Distributors (P) Ltd., 2004, pp. 66-67.

11. T. A Hussain 'Reopening of the Stilwell Road – Prospects of Solving Insurgency in the North-East', in D. Nath "*Reopening of the Stilwell Road: Prospects and Problems*" (ed), New Delhi, Anamika Publishers and Distributors (P) Ltd., 2004, p. 248.

12. Tuli Sinha 'Reviving the Stilwell Road: Challenges and Opportunities for India' Institute of Peace and Conflict Studies, Issue Brief, New Delhi, March 2010.

13. Lu Xun 'My Old Home', cited in Rob Gifford 'China Road: One Man's Journey into the Heart of Modern China', Bloomsbury, UK, 2007, p. 314.

PART I

2
Stilwell Road: A Historical Retrospect

D. Nath

Well-known today as Stilwell Road after World War II, the famous travel route between India and Burma up to Kunmimg in China, was the ancient migration route used by peoples of this part of the world for their cross-regional movements. Named variously as *Ledo Road* (from the Burmese side), *Bhamo Road* (from the Indian side), *Assam-Burma Route*, *Old Bisa Road*, *Old Opium Tract*, it was also known as the *Southern Silk Route*. This road connects India at the Pangsau Pass on the Patkai, about 3727 feet high, with Burma. Identified from the point of Ledo in the Tinsukia District of Assam, the road runs for about 61 km inside India and is well built up to a certain distance. Of this Indian part, a portion lies in Assam while the rest runs through Arunachal Pradesh. Beyond Pangsau Pass on the Patkai this ancient route runs through Burma for a long distance; firstly southerly, and then in a North-Easten direction spanning over more than a thousand kilometers till it reaches Muse (Mong-Yu), where it enters the Yunnan state of China and goes up to its capital, Kunming.

I

Early Historical Evidence

There are evidences of both Indian and Chinese origin to the effect that there was an old land route across the Patkai connecting India with the Yunnan state of China through Upper Burma, passing over the territories of Hukwang, Myitkina and Bhamo. The earliest mention of this route is to be found in the report of Changkien, a Chinese ambassador sent to the Yueh-chi country at Bactria, who submitted his report in the year 126 A.D.[1] Changkien had noted that he had seen silk and bamboo at Bactria which had been imported from Yunnan and Szechuan. It was reported to him that merchants carried them in their caravans through India.[2]

Hiuen Tsang who visited Kamarupa (Assam) in the middle of the 7th century A.D. has noted that King Bhaskaravarmana (594-650 A.D.) gave him the option to use any of the routes, land or sea, if he desired to return to his homeland via Kamarupa. The pilgrim has further noted that to the east of Kamarupa there were a series of hills and hillocks without any principal city; but one could reach through these hills and hillocks the south-west barbarians of China. He also mentioned the similarity of physiognomy among the people of this region across the hills and dales. According to him the south-west borders of Szechuan were distant, about a two-month's journey. The mountains were hard to pass; there were pestilential vapours and poisonous snakes and herbs.[3] Hiuen Tsang's account indicates that there was constant intercourse between India and China through Assam, although the passage routes were full of dangers and difficulties.

HiuenTsang's refers to a Yunnan-Burma overland route in the middle of the 7th century A.D. which ran from Tonkin to Kamarupa and from Kamarupa to Magadha.[4]

A description of this route at the close of the 8th century A.D. is found in the Chia Tan (Kia tan), where it is stated that the route started from Tonkin in southern China and passed through Yunnansen and Yunnanfou. Going westward therefrom it crossed the Salouen river and reached Chou-ko-leng to the east of Momein, between Shiveli and the Salouen. The route bifurcated there – one branch going towards the south-west reached Si-li, midway between Ta-guang and Mandalay. It then passed through Tou-min (Pagan) and reached Prome, the capital of Burma, and passing through the mountains of Aracan, entered Kamarupa (Assam). The other branch passed westward to Teng Chong (Momein) and crossing the Mi mountain reached Li-Shouei on the Irrawady, near Bhamo. It then proceeded further and crossing the river Longtsiuan (Magaung) passed through the town of Nagansi and then crossed the river Min-no (Chindwin). Beyond the Min-no it passed through a range of mountains and entered Kamarupa (Assam).[5] P.C. Bagchi states that viewed from India, this route started at Pataliputra, and then running through Kajangola (Rajmahal) and Pundarvardhana (North Bengal), reached Kamarupa (Assam). From Assam there were three routes leading to Burma: one by the valley of the Brahmaputra through the Patkai range and then through upper Burma. The second goes through Manipur, while the third passes through the Aracan hills.[6] All these routes, according to Bagchi, met on the frontier of Bhamo, and then proceeded over the mountains and across the river valleys of Unnanfu (Kunneing) which was the city of the southern province of China.[7]

G. Tucci has referred to a 16th century Buddhist monk from India named Buddhagupta, who, according to Tucci, mentions in his biography about the existence of a well-known land route between Assam and Burma.[8]

Understanding the existence of an overland route since centuries before Christ, Paul Pelliot has put its existence as far back as the second century B.C. in the reign of the Chinese emperor Wu-ti (140-87 B.C.)[9] Existence of this route since early times has been testified also by cross-country ethnic elements dated to a remote past.[10]

II

In the Assamese and Shan chronicles we find mention of the use of this overland route by Sukapha, the founder Ahom king of Assam, in the early 13th century; the narrative given therein is the most exhaustive and detailed of all the records so far obtained. This is recorded by the Assamese chronicles as well as by the Shan chronicles of Burma. These chronicles mention that Sukapha started from Kiang-sen Mao-lung, the capital city of Mong Mao to Assam (known to them as Mong-pa-kam). This Kiang-sen-Mao lung was located on the right bank of the river Nam Mao (Shweli).[11] It is narrated that Sukapha and his followers left Mong Mao and took a northerly route through Mong Wan, Mong Na, Mong Ti, and then followed a westerly route and arrived at Ta waing Mien (present Waing Mao) on the left bank of the Nam Kiu (Irrawady), nearly opposite to Myitkyina. This route, according to scholars, was largely used by the Shans of the Chinese Shan states of Mong La, Mong Santa, Mong Yin and others, until the close of the 18th century.[12] Crossing the river Nam Kiu at Ta Waing Mien, Sukapha is recorded to have further advanced towards the west when he and his men arrived at Mong Kwang (Mogaung). Then they passed through territories like Ban Lak, Che Kou, Mo' la- khong, Mong Khao, Mong pan, Phake che rin, and a series of hills thereafter. The team then arrived at the Khamjang valley on the bank of the Namjang Lake, just below the Pangsau Pass towards the southwest. Here Sukapha stayed for a few years till he brought the area under his consolidation. He then crossed the Patkai and entered the Dihing valley.[13] Thus, when one tries to prepare a sketch map of Sukapha's route as recorded by the chronicles, one finds his route to be as follows: Mao lung – Shiewli river – Mong wan- Mong na – Mong ti- Waing Mien – Namkiu river – Mong Kwang (Mugaung/ Mungkhang of Assamese chronicles) – Ban lak-Che Kou – Mong La khong – Mong Khao – Mong Pan – Phake che rin (the land of the Tai Phakes called as Phakial in Assam) – a series of hills called Doi Kham – Khamjang-Nongyang Lake – Pangsau Pass – Dihing Valley – Namrup. This shows that Sukapha followed the Ledo Namrup Pangsu Pass – Myitkyina route.

As recorded in the Assamese chronicles, in the period after Sukapha, this route was in constant use by the brother states of Assam and northern Burma and southern China.

Assamese chronicles further maintain that this route was in use for various purposes like migration of people, culture contact, and maintenance of political and diplomatic relations between Assam and Burma – throughout the centuries – till at least the decline of the Ahom state in the late 18th and early 19th century. It is recorded that after establishment of his hold over upper Assam with its centre of administration at Charaideo in the mid-13th century, when Sukapha sent an emissary to inform his brother king Su khan Pha in Mong Mao about his achievements in Assam. Sukapha's act was duly responded to by his brother with a similar emissary with presents of articles of value.[14] Such relationships continued during the time of the later Ahom rulers also and through the same route.[15] The route was in use till the beginning of the 19th century for maintenance of politico-diplomatic relations between the Ahom state and the various Shan states of northern Burma, like Mong Kwang (Mogaung). It was also used by various immigrant ethnic groups like the Khamti, Phakial and Singpho, to migrate to the Brahmaputra Valley during this period.[16]

III

In the early years of the 19th century the Burmese invaded Assam (1817, 1818, 1821) through this route.[17] As a result, the British, after occupation of Assam in the year 1826, initiated a series of investigations into the route used by the Burmese army to invade Assam. Such investigations were undertaken by Captain Neufville (in the year 1825), an army officer, to be followed by Lt. Burnet in 1828, William Griffith, a botanist, and Captain S.F. Hannay during 1836-37. Reports thus received revealed to the British that "There was an open road from upper Assam into Burma, and thence to China, by which a considerable amount of trade in Chinese and Burmese manufactures is carried on.... The line of trade after leaving Siddiya passes by Bisa across the Patkai range of mountains and through the valley of Hookoong, to the town of Moongkoong."[18] As a result, further investigation ensued, and H.L. Jenkins and S.E. Peal, tea planters from Jaipur, travelled through the route and produced reports on it in the years 1869 and 1879 respectively. A few years later, upper Burma came under the British rule in the year 1885. Since then they employed every effort to explore various overland routes between India, Burma and China; but nothing significant was done till the close of the World War II when in the face of Japan's advance towards Assam after occupying Burma and consequent blockade of the channels of supply China-based American General Joseph Stilwell, also known as Vinegar Joe (1883-1946) Commanding General of all US Forces in China, Burma and India, and Chief of Staff under Shiang Kai Shek of all Allied Armies of the Chinese Theatre of Operations, rebuilt it for carriage of coal and other war materials for the Allied Forces, rebuilt it for carriage of coal and other war materials for the Allied Forces. When ordered to prepare plans for that, General Joseph W. Stilwell's Operation Officer D. Merril recommended the building of a road from Ledo in Assam, south and east across northern Burma to a junction with the Old Burma Road, east of Bhamo. It was hoped that the proposed road would support a north-Burma campaign and, when linked with the old provide a land-supply line to China.[19] The work started from Ledo, and on 16 December, 1942, they began building the double track all-weather Ledo Road. The progress of the work was naturally slow due to so many constraints, natural hazards etc. But by the beginning of the year 1943 engineers were working round-the-clock, and in February they reached the Pangsau Pass, and at the close of the month they reached the Burmese border. However, progress of work was still slow. Therefore General Stilwell replaced Arrowsmith who was in charge of building the road by Colonel Lewis A. Pick who took over the charge in October, 1943. It was under his supervision that the work made quick progress, and on 27 December, 1943, it reached Singbwang, five days ahead of schedule. Thus about 117 miles of the road, from Ledo to Singbwang, now became open before January, 1944. Since then the work was in constant progress, and within 27 January, 1945, the road became complete and open.[20] Reporting that event of completion of this historic road James W. Dunn has recorded as follows,

It was none too soon for General Pick who, on 12 January, had led the first convoy out of Ledo, bound for Kunming, China. The 113 vehicles, driven by representatives of all the engineer units that had worked on the road, consisted of heavy cargo trucks, jeeps, and ambulances. Among the passengers were some 65 radio, magazine, and newspaper correspondents. The convoy reached Myitkyina on 15 January, where it stayed until 23 January because of the tactical situation. On 28 January, Pick led the convoy into Wanting where T.V. Soong, the Chinese Minister of Foreign Affairs, welcomed him. On 4 February, the convoy reached Kunming as fire crackers exploded, missionary nuns waved, and Chinese bands played. That night the Governor of Yunnan Province gave a banquet with American operatic star Lily Pons and her husband, conductor Andre Kostelanetz, in attendance. Pick's congratulatory message to his command expressed his sincere appreciation and pride in their achievement....

Finally, on 20 May 1945, newly promoted Major General Pick announced formal completion of the Ledo Road, a task he called the toughest job ever given to U.S. Army engineers during wartime. Renamed the Stilwell Road at the suggestion of Chiang Kai-shek, it was known to the engineers who built it as 'Pick's Pike.[21]

It is recorded that all the available local labour force, consisting of the tribes of the region from Ledo to Kachin, were employed in the building work; and the US, China, South Africa, Britain and India joined hands in the project making a total cost of 173 million US dollars being spent on the part from Ledo to Myitkyina.[22]

The road thus built was in full use for about one and a half years. After the close of World War II, its importance diminished as a route for emergency and military transport. In 1947, India attained independence, followed by Burma in 1949. The two independent countries have since closed the border portion of the road for reasons of security. Thus, it remains closed for the last half a century although unofficial socio-economic intercourse still remains a natural phenomenon in the region.

Environmental Condition of the Route

Narratives of the topographic condition of the route from Mytkynina to Ledo across the Patkai has been given by various sources since at least the 13th century onwards, the time of the coming of Sukapha to Assam. Records of the early centuries are to be found in the Assamese chronicles, while those of the 19th and early 20th centuries are found in British records. In both the sources it has been emphasized that both river and land routes were in use from across the Patkai to arrive at the plains of Assam. Sukapha is recorded to have used bamboo rafts on the Dihing river to come down to the plains due mainly to the thickly wooded jungle that spanned the region and prevented the sun's rays from penetrating that area.[23] Beyond the surroundings of the Nongyang Lake and the Khamjang area, there was no human settlement across the Pangsau Pass; and Sukapha had to engage his men to climb up the high trees and beat drums to know about any habitation.[24] There was no doubt that he brought his luggage on the backs of horses and elephants.[25] Assamese chronicles point to the fact that while these animals proceeded through the overland passage, Sukapha proceeded on rafts across the Dihing.[26]

The environment faced by Sukapha did not change much during the six hundred years of Ahom rule in Assam. The Shan chronicles of the early 19th century record the environment of this route. Chang Ang, a chicftain of village Mung Yang, who had accompanied the Burmese contingent during their invasion of Assam in the year 1817, has stated in his account that it took two weeks from his village to reach Mung kwang. The army had to pass through dense forests and marshes and cross many streams and rivers. Their soldiers had suffered painful water sores having to march through malarial terrain, across hills, muddy swamps. He wrote, "Of all the mountains we crossed over, the Patkai happened to be the highest one. To reach the top of it, one was to climb over as many as eighteen ridges, of which nine were quite big. It was from the summit that one should see altogether five roads girdling around the mountain and passing through numerous rocks. Climbing the mountain was so strenuous and taxing that one used to get exhausted with profuse perspiration all over the body at every step taken upward. We had to go on scaling our way continuously for twelve days. And, at the end of our suffering, we arrived at the bank of the river Burhi

Dihing."[27] He further adds that the road was "quite hazardous and no less insidious. So many of the recruits fought shy of braving the journey. They started pleading that arms were scarce, and that there were none to look after their wives and children. In the same way others also took cue of offering excuses of one or the other kind."[28]

The environment as noted by the Assamese and the Shan chronicles remained almost the same till colonial times. Major Jenkins, while narrating his experience of travel to the Pangsu Pass from Makum in Upper Assam in the year 1869, has noted as follows,

> Started from Makoom in the morning. There is no road eastwards or southwards beyond this point, except the natural bed of the Dihing river.... Both banks of the river (Dihing) were covered with a forest of immense timber trees, and underneath the larger trees was a rank growth of jungle through which we could not have made our way, except for the tracks of wild elephants. Along these tracts, when it is necessary to leave the bed of the river, we could walk, and with a little cutting of the creeping and climbing plants, the ponies could be made to follow very well; but the tracks were neither high enough nor broad enough to admit of elephants with their loads passing along them. We continued our march up the Namrup (Dihing is called Namrup in the upper part).... until we reached the mouth of a small stream called Nambong, when we left the Namrup and waded up

the Nambong to the mouth of a still smaller stream (called Nunkee)... . Continued to wade up the Nunkee with slow uncertain steps, for the bed of this stream is composed of large round slippery boulders.

After travelling an hour up the stream, we left it and commenced the ascent of the Patkoi by a narrow and not very well marked path. The ascent was not steep; the ponies had no difficulty except when we came to a fallen tree or some other obstruction caused by the living jungle. The path was very nearly straight; there was hardly any attempt to lessen its steepness by altering its direction. As we ascended, the forest trees seemed to improve in size, and the undergrowth of jungle to be less thick. Of the timber trees common to Assam, I particularly noticed the Sam (artocarpus chaplasha) and the Mekahi. These trees average at least twelve feet in girth, and the latter grows to the height of 60 to 70 feet without a branch. On the summit I found a good deep soil covered with bamboos, canes, and forest trees growing luxuriantly, but not so rankly as in the plains below. Many of the plants and trees are common to the plains, others were new to me, particularly, a cane bearing an edible fruit, which I do not recollect having seen before.

"As far as I could see, there is a depression in the Patkoi Range at this point, and it is to be supposed that the Burmese would not have selected this for their main route to Assam, unless it had possessed considerable

> advantage over every other path."[29] Jenkins has commented that, "The only difficulties to be encountered on the road between Assam and Hookoong are caused by the denseness of the jungle. The intervening country is a wilderness consisting of a forest of many useful timbers of immense size... . The only paths by which man can move are the natural beds of rivers or mountain streams. It would be impossible to leave these channels, except for the tracks made in the jungle by herds of wild elephants."[30]

James W. Dunn in his essay 'The Ledo Road' records: "The proposed route for the road went through some of the most difficult terrain in the world. The triangular shaped territory of northern Burma included jungle covered mountains and swampy villages. It was virtually uninhabited with the major towns being nothing more than frontier posts. The mountains, offshoots of the Himalayas, were formidable land barriers that rose to heights of 8,000 to 10,000 feet. The Hukawng and Mogaung valleys were tropical rain forests, dark and silent, with matted undergrowth where the clearings were really swamps covered with elephant grass 8 to 10 feet tall."[31] According to Dr. Gordon Seagrave, the well-known surgeon of Burma, "This unattractive area was the ancestral home of the leech. He found three major types: big brown ones on the ground, red ones on the elephant grass, and green on the tree branches. While the leeches were pests, the malaria-bearing mosquitoes and typhus-carrying mites could be deadly in the absence of strict preventive medicine measures."[32]

Predominance of leech and their attack from above the tree tops was a feature still a few years hence when the part of the road inside India was covered with dense jungles and human travel was hazardous. The present author had that experience when he visited the Pangsau Pass in the year 2002.

While discussing the circumstances leading to that condition of a once regularly frequented route from both sides across the mountain, J.N. Phukan has pointed out that till at least the close of the 18th century, the route was maintained by the rulers of Mong Kwang who agreed to do this as a matter of the understanding with the Ahom king Sudangpha *alias* Bamuni Konwar (1397-1407) in the year 1401. This agreement of the year 1401, was working well till the emergence of Burma as an imperial power under the rule of Bodawpaya who subjugated all the independent Shan and other chieftains of the region and destabilized the power system there. As a result, there were large-scale movements of the people from across the border, and the Patkai-Hookoong route became desolate and unsafe.[33] Consequently, neither the Ahom state which has now been crippled by internal crisis and external aggressions, nor the Burmese Government being under colonial pressure, had enough time to look after it. Thus, as pointed out by Jenkins, the route has fallen "almost entirely into disuse on account of the posts having been one by one deserted."[34]

Importance of the Route as Realised

The importance of the route has been noted all through the

ages. As a passage of human migration this route has acted as the interweaving force between the countries of Asia in the past. Besides Buddhist monks from India and China, traders from northern India visited China and other countries through the Brahmaputra Valley using this ancient route. Most pre-Ahom ethnic communities of Assam today are descendents of people who had migrated to this part of India in the remote past who brought with them elements of their culture and language and mixed them up with those of the people here. Such migration has never ceased to occur. In the 13th century the Ahoms of the Tai Shans came and founded a kingdom here which gave the region its name *Assam*, its social structure, system of agriculture, and its political and social identity. Following them came the Singphos, the Khamtis, the Phakials, the Turungs and so forth during the late 18th and early 19th century. Thus the society of the border areas on both sides are peopled by members belonging to the same ethnic stocks. Referring to this aspect Pemberton has noted that, "A constant communication appears to be held between the Singphos on our frontier and those occupying the hills on the southern side of the Patkoyee as far as Hookong valley or old Beesa, from whence the present Assam Singphos emigrated, after leaving their original haunts near the head of the Irrawattee; it is also by the pass that trade is conducted which has for the last three years been carried on between the Singphos within our limits, and the inhabitants of the Hookong valley."[35] Even during the 20th century, the criss-crossing of people across the border has not been stopped. It is significant to note that the ethnic affinity of these people, irrespective of their settlement, has always acted as the catalyst for receiving people from either side of the border; and it is because of the fact perhaps that immigration here has never been treated as a threat to the society. This has been noted by the British administrators also as early as the 19th century itself. "If Assam is to be repopulated," wrote Jenkins, "it will be from the east. That the existing population has been mainly derived from this quarter, is shown by the language, customs, and physical appearance of the people."[36] It is to be noted that it was these people who now form the only group of inhabitants who bring back that old and powerful religion – Buddhism – to its motherland.

All records show that this Patkai route has an important rôle to play on the economy of the Brahmaputra Valley. It has been shown that rice culture in Assam has been a legacy of its relationship with the regions across the Patkai.[37] In this connection one should not forget that the route used by the silk traders from China contributed largely to the growth of silk and the silk industry in the upper Brahmaputra Valley which forms a very distinguished character of Assamese culture today. Although in the absence of local records, one cannot find out about the actual amount of dependence these people had on each other from across the mountain ranges, there is no doubt that trade and exchange was a regular feature between the people of China and its neighbours, Burma and Assam in particular. This is clear from all records dating back to colonial and pre-colonial times. Realising the economic importance of the route, Captain Charlton in 1835, noted that a good road would facilitate regional trade between China and its neighbouring British territories. He wrote, "What a pity there is no means of communication between Suddya and Yunnan. A good land road – and there are no natural obstacles of any consequence to prevent it – would afford an outlet for British merchandise into the very heart of China."[38] That trade and exchange still holds the key to our neighbourly relationship and economic progress has been aptly signified by the present cross-border daily life on the Pangsau Pass.[39]

As China, Burma and India, are contiguous regions the strategic or political importance of the route was always felt. It is to be noted that most of the state-forming tribes of Upper Assam had their base in either southern China or northern Burma. Scholars argue that the founders of the Chutiya kingdom in the extreme North-Eastern corner of the Brahmaputra Valley in the pre-Ahom times came from the China-Burma adjoining regions from where Samlungpha, a predecessor of Sukapha, came and conquered the Chutiyas in the early 12th century A.D.[40] The Chutiyas thereafter retraced further west and ruled over this part of the country for about three hundred years when in the year 1523, their state was occupied and annexed by the Ahom king Suhungmung *alias* Dihingia Raja (1497-1539)[41] The Chutiya kings not only extended their influence over this region, but also made political and diplomatic friendships with the kings of Kamata in the western Brahmaputra Valley and northern Bengal.[42] The Ahoms who succeeded the Chutiyas, ruled the

Brahmaputra Valley for six hundred years, and established their identity as a political power not only in the North-Eastern part of India, but also over the entire country. After the Ahoms, came the Singphos and the Khamtis – both of whom exercised significant political power in the 19th century history of this part of India.[43] For which the British had to formulate an exclusive tribal policy during their rule.[44] All this shows that the route across Patkai through the Pangsau Pass is significant enough to be taken into account for emerging India and its neighbours in the coming times. It was therefore not without reason that General Joseph Stilwell expended so much of time and money for renovating and rebuilding this road in the mid-20th century.

From the above historical account it becomes clear that human connection across natural and political barriers and boundaries was a natural phenomenon all through the ages. The Assam-Burma route through the Pansau Pass is one of the major human discoveries towards enhancement of such connectivity. As the Silk Road in the past, the Assam-Burma-China route in the Middle Ages, and the Stilwell Road in modern times, it has served men in all these ages seek, find and not yield and compromise with hurdles in the formation of their civilizations in this part of the world. Significantly, every human group carried from their homeland human habits, language and culture, and above all, fabrics of their civilizations. Society here therefore shares a common heritage; a heritage that we all claim. This is why the importance of this route has never been challenged by any force, political or otherwise, at any period of time in the long history of mankind. It is therefore not likely that the rebuilding and renovation of this road was initiated only by General Stilwell and that too in the mid-20th century; there were invariably earlier attempts, although it might be in a different form not much appreciated by our modern minds. King Sukapha's travel from Maolung in the year 1215, and his arrival at Charaideo forty years after, duly consolidating his position on the way, points to this fact. The conclusion of a treaty on the Patkai Pass between the kings of Assam and Mugaung in the year 1401, and the responsibility fixed for both of them therein to maintain the route, is the next historical example about it. If, according to Peal, the Burmese Government before the colonial rule, put one village or an outpost every twelve-fifteen miles apart, along the route to take care of it, to cut down the jungles and cleanse the road and remove any obstructions from the path to allow free movement,[45] then it was a constant endeavour on the part of the people inhabiting around it to renovate and rebuild it from time to time. Stilwell's endeavour in the mid-20th century, therefore, is a part of the whole historical process of our advancement in civilizations.

Notes and References

1. Cited by B.K. Barua, in his *A Cultural History of Assam*, Vol. I, Lawyer's Book Stall, Gauhati, 1969, p. 110.
2. Ibid.
3. S. Beal (tr.) *Buddhist Records of the Western World*, London, K. Paul, Trench, Trubner and Co., 1905, pp. 198f.

4. T. Watters (tr.), *On Hiuen Tsang's Travels in India,* Vol. II, Hesperides Press, London, 1908, pp. 195f.; also Pelliot, *Bulletin de l'Ecole Francaise d'Extreme Orient*, Vol. IV, pp. 131f; R.C. Majumdar, (ed.), *The Classical Age*, Bombay, Bharatiya Vidya Bhavan, 4th edition, 1988, pp. 599fn.
5. cf. P.C. Bagchi, *India and China: A Thousand years of Cultural Relations*, Bombay, 1950, pp. 18ff.
6. Ibid, p. 19.
7. Ibid, p. 19.
8. 'The Sea and Land Travels of a Buddhist Sadhu in the Sixteenth Century, in the *Indian Historical Quarterly*, Vol. VII, pp. 683ff.
9. Deux itineraries de Chine en Inde a la fin du VIIe siècle, *Bulletin de l' ecole francaise d' extreme-Orient*, IV, 1904, pp. 142f.
10. Also see B.S. Guha, *An outline of the Racial Ethnology of India*, Calcutta, Indian Science Congress Associations, 1937, for details.
11. J.N. Phukan has stated, "In accordance with the Chinese policy towards the minority nationalities the former Tai states of Mong Mao, Mong Wan, Mong Na, Santa, and several other localities are constituted into an autonomous prefecture. This prefecture is called *Dehong Tai-Singpho Autonomous Prefecture* (Dehong Daizu Jingpo Zhizhizou) with its capital at Mangshi (properly Mong Se), called Luxi by the Chinese." cf. D. Nath, (ed.), *Reopening of the Stilwell Road: Prospects and Problems*, Calcutta, MAKAIAS, 2004, p. 44).
12. *Gazetteer of Upper Burma and the Shan States*, Part II, Vol. II, p. 567; cf. J.N. Phukan, loc. cit.
13. For details see *Deodhai Asam Buranji* (ed. S.K. Bhuyan), 2nd edition, Department of Historical and Antiquarian Studies (DHAS), Government of Assam, Guwahati, 1962, pp. 7ff; *Ahom Buranji* translated into English by G.C. Baruah, Spectrum, Reprint, 1985, pp. 44f.
14. S.K. Bhuyan, ed. *Deodhai Asam Buranji*, pp. 8f; J.N. Phukan et al. (ed). *Chao-lung Siu-ka-pha: Documentary History of the Ahom*, vol. I, 1998, pp. 18f.

15. See *Satsari Asam Buranji*, 2nd edition, 1964, p. 7.

16. See W. Robinson, *A Descriptive Account of Assam*, (1841), Reprint, Delhi, Sanskaran Prakashak, 1975, pp. 371ff.

17. *Waissalisa*, op. cit, pp. 19ff.

18. John M'Cosh, *Topography of Assam*, 1837, Reprint, New Delhi, Logos Press, 1986, p. 11

19. James W. Dunn, 'The Ledo Road' in Leslie Andres, *Ledo Road: General Joseph W. Stilwell's Highway to China*, Oklahoma University, Oklahoma, 1965, p. 329

20. Ibid., pp. 336ff.

21. Ibid., pp. 345f.

22. *Stilwell Papers*, Cf. Pradip Hazarika, 'The Stilwell Road: The (A) Saga of Grit and Swan Song of (the) Future' in D. Nath (ed.), op. cit, p. 101.

23. *Deodhai Asam Buranji*, op. cit, p. 7f, 99f; *Ahom Buranji*, op. cit, pp. 24ff.; *Satsari Asam Buranji*, Reprint, Gauhati University, S.K. Bhuyan (ed.), 1964, p. 3ff.

24. Ibid.

25. There is conflicting information about the horse and elephant strength taken by Sukapha with him in his march to the Brahmaputra Valley. But the most plausible explanation may be that he brought a force of a few elephants and about three hundred horses. Of the companions of Sukapha, most of them were men; and very few were women. It is recorded that Sukapha's men took women as their wives only in Assam. See ibid; also Hiteswar Barbarua, *Ahomar Din*, Publication Board, Assam, Guwahati, 1981, pp. 456f.

26. Ibid.

27. *Weissalisa*, (tr.) B. Barua, (ed.), M. Bora, Dibrugarh University, 1977, p. 9f.

28. Ibid.

29. 'Notes on the Burmese Route from Assam to the Hookoong Valley' in 1869-70, cf. *Selection of Papers Regarding the Hill Tracts between Assam and Burmah and on the Upper Brahmaputra*, Government of Bengal, 1873, Reprint, 1981, pp. 250ff.

30. Ibid., p. 253.

31. cf. Leslie Andres, op. cit, p. 329.

32. Ibid.

33. op. cit, p. 47.

34. Jenkins, op. cit, p. 253.

35. *Report on the Eastern Frontier of British India* (1835), Reprint, DHAS, Gauhati, 1966, p. 72.

36. Jenkins, loc. cit, p. 254.

37. See Amalendu Guha, *Medieval and Early Colonial Assam-Polity, Society and Economy*, K.P. Bagchi, Calcutta, 1991, p. 61ff.

38. cf. Jenkins, loc. cit.

39. Also see H. Goswami and J.K. Gogoi, 'Economic Prospects of the Stilwell Road: An Analysis', in D. Nath ed. op. cit, p. 109ff.

40. See Ney Elias, *Introductory Sketch of the History of the Shans in Upper Burma and Western Yunnan*, Foreign Department Press, Calcutta, 1876, p. 61ff; S.L. Barua and D. Nath (ed.), *Chutiya Buranji*, All Assam Chutiya Sanmilan, Guwahati, 2006, p. 104ff.

41. See E.A. Gait, *A History of Assam*, 2nd edition Reprint, Lawyer's Book Stall, Gauhati, 1981, pp. 86f.

42. See K.L. Barua, *Early History of Kamarupa*, Lawyer's Book Stall, Gauhati, 1966, pp. 161ff.

43. See W. Robinson, op. cit, pp. 371ff.

44. See R.B. Pemberton, *Report on the Eastern Frontier of British India*, for details

45. Peal, 'Note on the Old Burma Route over Patkai via Nongyang' in *JASB, XXXXIII*, Part II, pp. 69ff.

3
The Lost Trail: The Stilwell Road in Historical and Contemporary Scenarios

Lipi Ghosh

Inter-Asian linkages and connectivity are important subjects for modern-day research. When we talk of inter-Asian linkages, we move beyond national borders, and transcend many political boundaries. North-East India is a region from where we can identify many trans-national linkages. While we talk of North-East India's outside linkage, we have enough proof to establish the existence of a direct trade route between North-East India and South-west China, over historical periods. There are several historical records from the ancient, medieval and colonial periods which confirm the existence of a direct trade link between North-East India and South-west China through a specific road, i.e. the Stilwell Road.

The Stillwell Road falls within the parameter of the Southern Silk Road, an ancient and relatively unknown trade route that linked the south-western Chinese provinces of Sichuan and Yunnan to eastern India. This present paper is an attempt at understanding the historical and contemporary settings of this road, namely the Stilwell Road.

An aerial view of the Ledo Road. http://www.google.com/images?stilwell+road accessed on 22 May, 2010)

Historian H.P. Ray speaks about the route from China to North-East India. From Yunnan in China the road from Yongchang (Baoshan) of the Ailao kingdom in Yunnan was historically a gateway to the outside world, where merchants from home and abroad traded. Historical records describe this prefecture in the first century A.D. (Mingdi reign, 58 to 75 A.D.) as having eight countries and sixty thousand households, being 6900 *li* (3400 kms) from Luoyang (the national Capital of China) and situated at the extreme south-west end of Ningzhow. In this entire prefecture there lived the Minpos, Yues, Indians (Sendu or Zhuandu) and other nationalities like Jiaoluo or Gelo (the Garos).

It had flourishing commerce and produced a great variety of commodities. Tengcheng was an equally important place for domestic and foreign trade. Within the boundaries of Burma, Bhamo and Myitkyina were equally important centres of trade and served as links between India in the west and China in the east. Inside the Brahmaputra Valley, one could travel both by land and by water routes, passing through Sadiya, Kapili (near present-day Nowgong), Pragjyotishpura (Guwahati), Hadapeswara (Tezpur). Guwahati being in the middle reaches of the Brahmaputra was the capital of the ancient powerful kingdom of Kamrupa and enjoyed a strategic position, joining the Burma trade route in the east and feeding it to the northern areas, in the west.[1]

There are detailed records of the roads and mileages from Dali to Burma and India dating back to the 7th century. The Xin Tangshu (*The New History of the Tang Dynasty*) *Dili Zhi chapter* (Geography) gives the distance from present-day Dali to the ancient city of Tagaung in Burma as 700 kms where the city of Pyu (Pagan, ancient Burmese kingdom) was 500 kms away. Thence Kamarupa, located at the lower and middle courses of the Brahmaputra river was 800 kms to the west of Pundravardhana (in northern Bengal, 200 kms away and Magadha on the south bank of the Ganga 300 kms away).[2]

When we talk about the Tai-Azhom linkage, we find that the Ahoms of Assam, also known as Tai-Shans (the Burmese called the Tais from China on the northern Burmese border as Shans) followed this old route through the Patkai range from Maulung in China, then passed over to the Hukong valley in Upper Burma, and arrived at Tipam, near the coal town of Mergharita in the eastern Brahmaputra Valley, around 1252 A.D. (See map showing ancient trade route from South and South-west China to North-East India and beyond, through Northern Myanmar (Burma) and Northern Assam's Patkai Range).

In fact, the Ahom migration to Assam is convincing proof of the constant use of the North-Eastern route to China. Sukapha, the leader of the Ahoms, was not the first to follow the Patkai route. It is learnt from Assamese sources that some Mao-Shans (sometime in the 6th century A.D.) crossed the Sri Lohit (Irrawaddy) and entered the country called Prophangpau (Puphangpom), which might be somewhere in the northern foothills of the Patkai, and subduing the native people, they consolidated the power of the Mao-Shans there.[3]

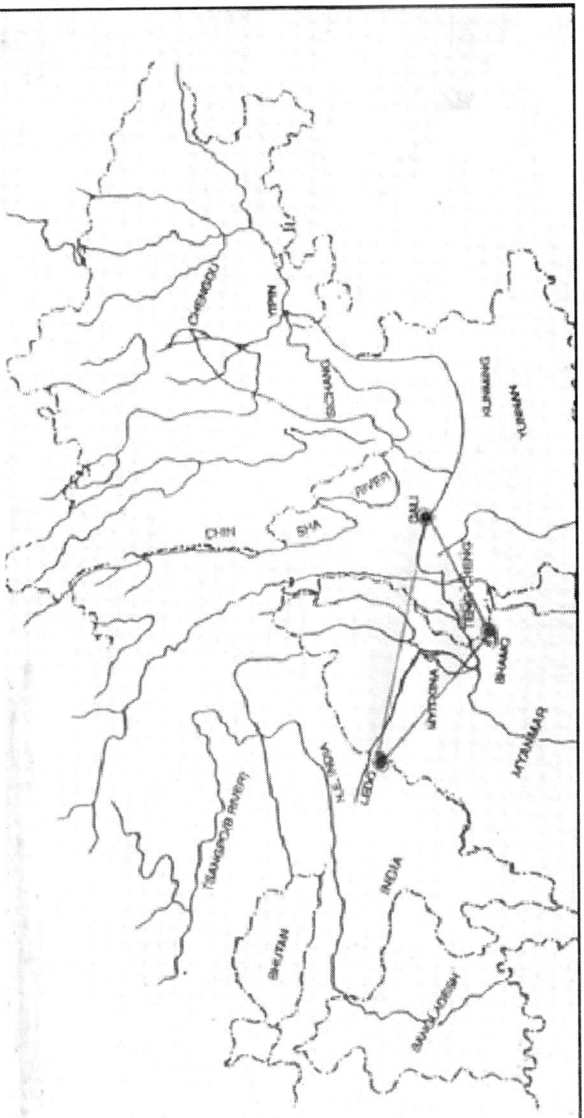

Ancient Trade Route from South & Southwest China to Northeast India and beyond, through Northern Myanmar (Burma) and Northern Assam's Patkai Range

Khun Lung (586 A.D. to 638 A.D.), one of the two ancestors of the Tai-Ahoms ruled over a vast empire extending from Chiangmai in Northern Siam in the east to the vicinity of the Lohit (Brahmaputra) in the west.[4] It is possible that during this period some Tais and also non–Tais, like the Mons and the Chinese, have migrated to North-East India through the Patkai Pass. These immigrants possibly took the shortest route to the Patkai. But for the Ahoms led by Sukhapha having mainly followed the river courses, the route of their migration was possibly not exactly the same as the one followed by these people.

The hazardous journey from Upper Burma to Upper Assam via the Patkai hills is however learnt about in detail from a later source. Chang Ang, the chieftain of the village Moung Yang, who accompanied the Burmese contingent in its first invasion of Assam in 1817 A.D., has left a comprehensive account of the advance of the army from Moung Kwang till its arrival at Charaideo (Jorhat/ Sibsagar), the then capital of the Ahoms, via the Patkai Pass. The chronicle is written in the Tai-Ahom language and is titled *Weissali* (Assam). *ukong*.[5] According to this source, it took two weeks to reach Moung Khong (Moung Kham) from Moung Yang, via Moung Kong.

During the colonial period part of this road, the stretch between Bhamo and Dali, regained some additional importance while the British and the French were involved in colonial competitions to capture the south China trade. The history of French and British explorations to capture

South China trade routes makes an interesting study. [6] For the British, who were in occupation of Lower Burma, the South China trade routes contemplated a prosperous trade network from China to Chittagong via Upper Burma. They had a plan to get access by a shortcut route from Bhamo in Upper Burma to Dali in the Yunnan province of Southern China and to fulfil their ambition, they finally annexed Upper Burma in 1885.

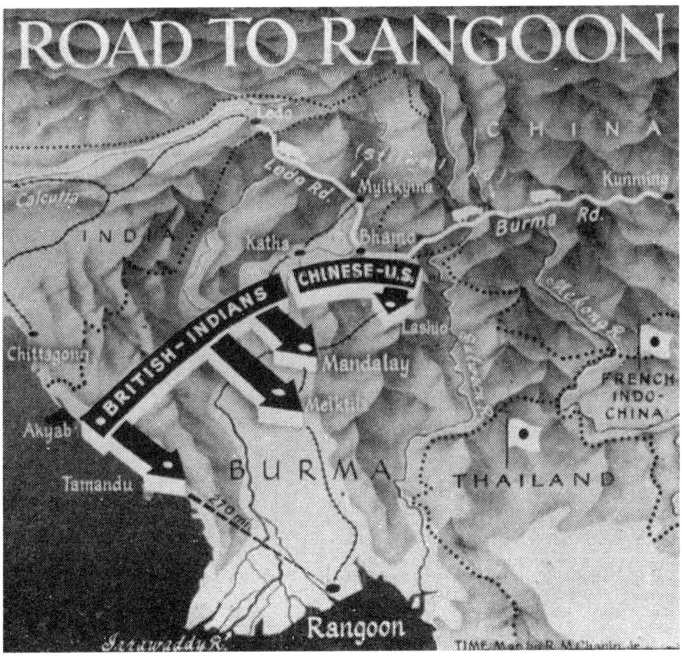

(1) World War II map of the Stilwell Road, China-Burma-India theatre

Donovan Webstar's study shows how this ancient road was revived when World War II entered a crucial stage in early 1940. Japan had cut China off from all maritime contacts. At that juncture the Indo-Chinese (or Sino-Indian) highway, renamed after the American General as the Stilwell Highway, carved out the lifeline for China for receiving arms, food and other supplies routed from India. It was this vital link between India and China which won the anti-Japanese war. It was built six feet wide to make room for American one-tonners. The first truck plied on the road in October, 1944. For almost 16 months, unending convoys of the USA and other Allied countries passed along this road on their journey from Assam to China.[7]

(2) General Joseph W. Stilwell

(3) General Joseph W. Stilwell (right) and Major General Frank D. Merrill planning the mission to capture the airstrip in Myitkyina, Burma, during World War II

In modern times this Stillwell Road stretches from Ledo in Assam to Bhamo (Myanmar) and then proceeds to Kunming, across the Patkai range. From Kunming, Chinese railway lines spread all over China. From Ledo to Kunming the road is of 1726 kilometres (1079 miles).

After Burma was liberated, the road gradually fell into disrepair. The last recorded vehicular journey from Ledo to Myitkyina and beyond (but not to China) was the Oxford-Cambridge Overland Expedition, which in 1955, drove from London to Singapore and back. For many years, travel into the region was restricted because of an active insurgency presence in the area. Because of continuous clashes between

(4) World War II stretches of the Stilwell Road, China-Burma-India theatre

Source for Pictures 1, 2, 3, and 4:

Source: http://www.google.co.in/images?hl=en&q=Stilwell+Road&um= 1&ie=UTF-8&source=univ&ei= CQEPTfnsLMLyrQfmn4 jFCw&sa=X&oi=im age_result_group&ct=title&resnum= 2&ved=0CDMQsA QwA Q&biw=1259&bih=775

insurgents (who were seeking shelter in Burma) and the Indian Armed Forces, India imposed harsh restrictions between 1962 and the mid-1990s on travel into Burma, a restriction that also applied to outsiders.

Table: Location-wise distance from Ledo, Assam, India to Kunming, Yunnan, China within the Ledo Road (Stilwell Road)

STILWELL ROAD (LEDO ROAD)		
Location	*Distance from Ledo, Assam, India*	
	in Kms	*in Miles*
Ledo	0	0
Pangsau Pass	61	38
Tagap Hill	127	79
Shindbwiyang	165	103
Jambu-Bum	287	178
Warazup	304	189
Myitkyina	403	250
Bhamo	595	372
Namkham	707	439
Mong-Yu (Ledo-Burma Roads junction)	749	465
Wanting*	811	507
Lungling*	896	560
Paoshan*	1,043	652
Yungpin*	1,208	755
Yunnanyi*	1,402	876
Tsuyung*	1,543	959
Kunming*	1,726	1,079
LENGTH OF ROAD LIES WITHIN		
INDIA	61	38
MYANMAR (BURMA)	1,033	646
CHINA	632	395

* Lies on the Burma Road.

Since the improvement of relations between India and Myanmar, travel has improved and tourism has begun near Pangsau Pass (at the Lake of No Return), but recent attempts to travel the full road have met with varying results. A book on an expedition to this area, written by Tim Slessor (1957), reported that bridges were down in the section between Pangsau Pass and Shingbwiyang. At present the Nampong-Pangsau Pass section is passable on four-wheel drive vehicles. The road on the Burmese side is now reportedly fit for vehicular traffic. Donovan Webster reached Shingbwiyang by road in 2001, and in mid-2005, veterans of the Burma Star Association were invited to join a 'down memory lane' trip to Shingbwiyang organised by a politically well-connected travel agent. These groups successfully travelled the road.

In the course of time, the Stilwell Road had virtually disappeared due to the fact that the road lies in the lands of three different nations, namely China, Burma and India and due to non-maintenance of the road by the respective nations. However, 61 km of the road lies in India, 1,033 km in Burma (Myanmar) and 632 km in China. In India out of the 61 km in Indian territory, 30 km lies in Assam and 31 km in Arunachal Pradesh. The border between Assam and Arunachal Pradesh has 14 km of this road section. Previously, this patch of road was in a deplorable condition. Now it has been repaired and the construction of an international trade route is under way, to link it with Myanmar at Pangsau Pass. On the Indian side, the road is being repaired and renovated up to Nampong under this scheme, and an extension of the renovation work up to Pangsau Pass, on the Indo-Myanmar border is under way. The section of road which lies within Arunachal Pradesh has been maintained by the Government of Arunachal Pradesh and the road section which lies within the area of Assam, of that 14 km, is being been maintained by the Government of Assam.

How to Reach the Stilwell Road (Ledo Road)

To reach Stilwell Road (Ledo Road), one starts out from Ledo, Assam, India, and passes through Jagun, Jairampur, Nampong, Pangsau Pass, Myanmar (Burma) and then up to Kunming, Yunnan Province, China. Ledo, the starting point of the road is connected to Dibrugarh airport, Tinsukia railway station and Margherita local railway station, which are the nearest locations to it. The Assam State Transport Corporation buses and Arunachal Pradesh State Transport buses ply daily from Dibrugarh and Tinsukia via Margherita.

Government of India Proposal

The Indian government has proposed the reopening of this road as an international highway-cum-trade route link to Myanmar (Burma), China and other South East Asian countries from India. The reopening of this road as a trade route will increase interaction among the people of the neighbouring countries and maintain good relationships

The Stilwell Road (Ledo Road)

Source: http://www.google.co.in/images?hl=en&q=Stilwell+Road&um=1&ie=UTF8&source=univ&ei=CQEPTfnsLMLyrQfmn4jFCw&sa =X&oi=image_result_group&ct=title&resnum=2 & ved=0CDMQsAQwAQ&biw=1259&bih=775

among the member countries. It will also boost trade and attract inland and foreign tourists as the road itself is historically famous and significant due to its close link with the World War II, which in turn will boost the socio-economic development of this most backward border area and will benefit the local people.

Everyone in this area is looking forward to the implementation of the project within the stipulated time and hoping for the area to be established as a major international trade centre. We should take aggressive steps towards the development of this road project; otherwise China may overcome us in that region some day.

Hopeful of getting Myanmar's nod to re-open the historic Stilwell Road connecting India and China, the government has approved an alternative route via the Sitwee port in that country, which would open the North-East to the rest of South Asia. The Union DoNER Minister B.K. Handique told PTI.... Myanmar, "Though India wants to open the Stilwell Road, Myanmar has been opposing the idea, citing certain reasons. But we are hopeful that the road would open one day. As of now, an alternative route via the Sitwee port of Myanmar would open the North-East to the rest of South East Asia," DoNER sources said that Myanmar is not interested in opening the road as it passes through the country's Kachin region which is infested with insurgent elements, including those belonging to India, like the ULFA and the NSCN factions.[8]

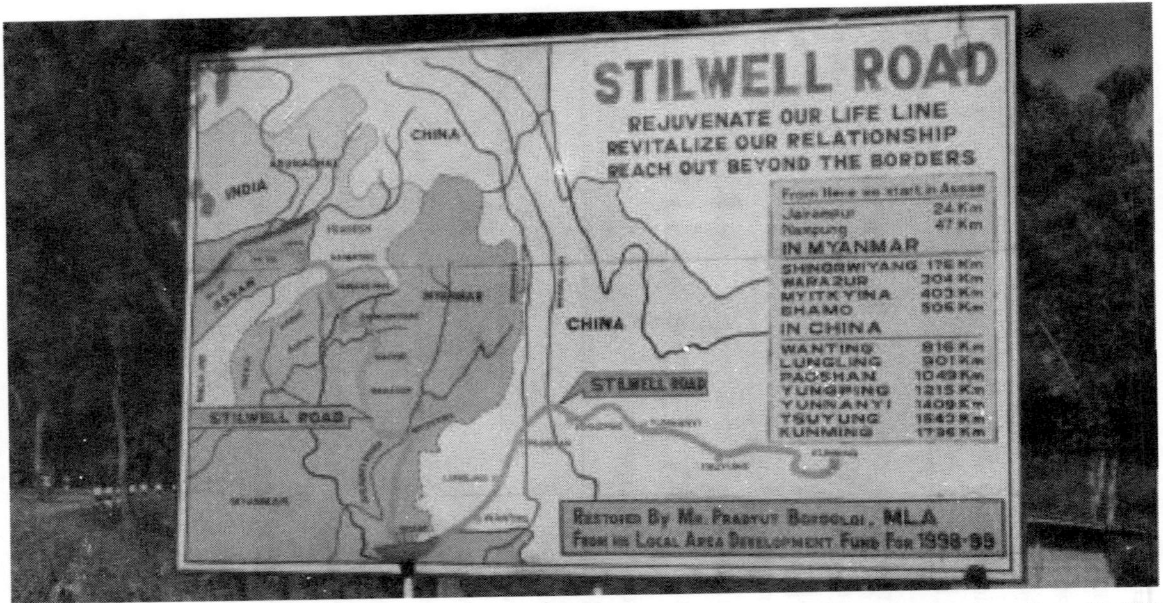

Source http://www.google.co.in images?hl=en&qStil well+Road &um= 1&ie=UTF8&source=univ&ei=CQEPT fnsLMLyrQfmn4jFCw&sa=X&oi=image_result_group&ct=title&resnum=2&ved=0C DMQsAQwA Q&biw=1259&bih=775

The whole question of the opening up of this route is to be reviewed in the context of emerging closer ties between India and China on the one hand and India and South East Asia on the other hand. Regarding China, over the last decade, the Joint Working Group (JWG) meetings between China and India have emerged as the most important platform for Sino-Indian dialogue. It is true that the JWG has not been able to address the resolution of the border problem, but given the complexity of the issue, it was not expected to arrive at an early solution. But the JWG had been moving gradually towards a point where both India and China would find a mutually agreed solution. To restore mutual trust and goodwill, both China and India must explore possible areas of cooperation. The coming together of China and India in their criticism of NATO actions in Yugoslavia and their forward venture in signing the agreement on the Trans-Asian Highway (which seeks to set up a railway line from Yunnan in China to Paris via Myanmar, Bangladesh, India and Pakistan) are good steps towards restoring faith and goodwill in Sino-Indian relations.[9]

The Tai-Ahom Historical Passageway: A Corridor for India-China-South East Asia Cooperation?

We proposed creation of a new Ledo-Bhamo-Dali Growth Triangle. This proposal is based on the premise that the North-East Indian passageway connecting the Indian subcontinent to East/South East Asia is believed to have been a major corridor for human migrations.

However, ethnic tension and concern over economic and resource exploitation in different parts of this region cannot be overcome overnight. But a stronger economy, free, accountable and just society is desirable by the people and may reduce tension. This will require working towards better management of resources, innovative management, and sustainable development which can be fostered in an accountable, transparent and democratic environment.

We need to think how this historic, age-old corridor, can be utilised to evolve the region into a zone of economic prosperity. We need to ask ourselves whether we would sincerely desire that this region needs to be a region of peace and prosperity. Otherwise this region will simply add to an already overburden of human misery and poverty in the region, due to its own helplessness, and neglect by the world community.

The people of North-East India have significant stakes in the trans-national sub-regional projects earmarked for the region. There is today a virtual boom in the construction of cross-national highways, roads, rail and air corridors thanks to the interest of multilateral organizations and advanced industrial countries with a stake in the globalized economy. Multilateral initiatives have brought together donor countries, land-locked developing countries and transit developing countries on infrastructure development, trade facilitation and regional cooperation projects. It can be assumed therefore, that the Stillwell Road may one day come within the purview of their interest.

Conclusion

This uppermost passage connecting China and South East Asia with India should be renovated as this road can facilitate international overland trade connecting China, Myanmar and other South East Asian countries to India, eventually moving down to the Bay of Bengal port of Haldia near Kolkata and thereby further boosting our business with the Indian Ocean littorals.

The inclusion of China in this Growth Triangle, as suggested by the Chinese, is very important. I propose the creation of the Ledo-Bhamo-Dali Growth Triangle, which eventually would result in an economic grid across the whole of mainland South East Asia. China's inclusion in the aforesaid proposed Growth Triangle is important to reassert the golden historical Tai-Ahom linkage from southern China. For China, their priority is the Kunming Initiative, which seeks to link up the Chinese province of Yunnan with Myanmar, Bangladesh and India's North-Eastern states, and eventually Thailand and other countries of mainland South East Asia, as an economic grid.

To achieve this end, both the governments at the Centre and at the state levels have to be forward looking and take initiative and concrete measures to promote India's foreign trade. We have identified pre-colonial cultural ties of North-East India with South East Asia. The pressing necessity of the day is to do away with the colonial 'super imposed' structure. The whole issue is to be addressed with multilateral or multi-cultural approaches. There should evolve a feeling of mutuality in trans-border transactions and there should be more and more tolerance towards our neighbours. The real notion of modernity demands a greater motivation towards accommodation and more openness in dealings towards 'the other'. This region can contribute tremendously to the nation's revenue if industry is properly developed and utilized both by government and private entrepreneurs, under the aegis of governmental support. It should be given developmental privileges as accorded to our existing Special Economic Zones and thus we can look forward to a prosperous future. Let our attitude of modernity result in a very viable inter-regional cooperation, collaboration and amity.

References

1. Haraprasad Ray, *Trade and Trade Routes between India and China*, Kolkata, Progressive Publisher's, 2003, p. 75: Hence forth *Trade Routes*.

2. Ibid.

3. Pushpadhar Gogoi as quoted in Haraprasad Ray, *Northeast India's Place in India-China Relations and its Future Role in India's Economy*, Kolkata, Institute of Historical Studies, 2003, p. 113.

4. N. Elias, *Introductory Sketch of the History of the Shans in Upper Burma and West Yunnan*, Calcutta, Foreign Department Press, 1876, p.18.

5. H.P. Ray, op.cit. p. 114.

6. For details see Lipi Ghosh, *Burma: Myth of French Intrigue*, Kolkata, Naya Udyog, 1994, pp 104-136.

7. For details see Donovan Webster, *The Burma Road: The Epic Story of One of World War II's Most Remarkable Endeavours*, London, 2003.

8. "Centre Hopes to Re-open Historic Stilwell Road", Shillong / *Press Trust of India*, Thu-Jun 25, 2009.

9. Bhartendu Kumar Singh, Sino-Indian Ties: The 11th Round of Joint Working Group Meeting, Institute of Peace & Conflict Studies, New Delhi, Article No. 195, 7 June, 1999.

4
India-China Relations: No Need to Over Hype the Connectivity Factor

D.S. Rajan

The term 'connectivity' has a positive connotation; it cannot be disputed that connectivity between India and China contributes to better mutual understanding among them, which in turn will positively influence their policies towards each other. One cannot miss the fact that the two nations presently enjoy a high degree of connectivity, encompassing a variety of fields – say political, economic, military and cultural. People-to-People contacts do need further strengthening. What has led to such a connectivity surge? It can be seen without difficulty that the main contributing factor has been the congruence, to a good degree, of strategic interests among China and India, which gradually came about over the years in response to the profound geo-political transformation, witnessed both at global and regional levels. e.g. end of the Cold War, post- 9/11 situation, etc.

The term 'congruence' may need elaboration. China – especially since 1978, when reforms began – is following a strategy aimed at guaranteeing the success of its modernisation programme under conditions of a 'peaceful international environment' and a 'stable neighbourhood'; an offshoot of this strategy has been a foreign policy based on a 'harmonious world' concept providing for a win-win relationship with the rest of the world, including India. China at the same time explains that it is still a developing nation and its international role will be within its capacity, meaning thereby that it does not intend to play a domineering role in world affairs. On its part, India under its reform path, initiated in the early 80s, is also linking its development requirement with 'peace and stability' in the region; a concept of economic linkages with the outside world, especially with China and other East Asian nations, has been introduced by it accordingly. India's Look East Policy has been its specific manifestation. From the point of view of an international relations theory, academicians may see that the courses undertaken by India and China fall under the 'Realism School' which gives primacy to national interests.

It is not surprising that the India-China congruence of interests has resulted in a substantial increase in comfort levels in their bilateral relations, especially since the time of the landmark visit of the then Indian Prime Minister Rajiv Gandhi to China, in 1988, which had resulted in the setting up of a Joint Working Group to address the border dispute. A series of significant events have influenced progress in bilateral relations after that. They include the appointment of Special

Representatives to explore the framework of a boundary settlement, from the political perspective of overall bilateral relation (2003) agreements, signed on 'Strategic and Cooperative Partnership for Peace and Prosperity and Political Parameters and Guiding Principles for Settlement of the Boundary Question' (2005), 'Promotion of Civil Nuclear Cooperation (2006) and 'Shared Vision for the 21st Century' (2008).

India-China ties have now acquired a global character. Accordingly, the two nations are cooperating on international issues related to the diversification of a global energy mix, climate change, arms control and disarmament, non-traditional security threats, counter-terrorism, WTO, WMD, human rights and South-South Co-operation. Bilaterally, the two sides now aim at building 'a relationship of friendship and trust, based on equality, in which each is sensitive to the concerns and aspirations of the other'. They are not viewing each other as a security threat and by and large are satisfactorily implementing confidence building measures (CBMs) along the disputed border, besides carrying out joint military exercises. Special Representatives of India and China have so far held thirteen rounds of border talks, though with no tangible results. Most important is the attitude of promoting ties, and looking beyond the unsolved and 'complex' border dispute, India and China are speeding up their trade and economic contacts. Bilateral trade is fast gathering momentum, with the volume increasing to the tune of US$ 60 billion. China has emerged as India's largest trading partner, replacing the US, in the April 2008-February 2009 period. Also significant enough is the ongoing momentum in their exchanges of high level visits, reflecting the desire of each party to forge stronger ties, of which the recently concluded state visit of the Indian President Ms. Pratibha Patil to China is a prominent example.

We at the same time should not forget that for India and China, the connectivity factor entails some limitations; it may no doubt help in generating a positive atmosphere in India-China relations, but such an atmosphere, may not necessarily lead to eradication of the existing gaps in the respective strategic perceptions, which are based on self-interests. There have been some references in the talks to past civilisational contacts between the two nations helping in the resolution of the dividing issues between the two nations. But such arguments look invalid as the two nations, having emerged as modern nation states, have come to face geo-political compulsions, which tend to put one against the other.

On the matter of perceptional gaps, the position on the boundary issue comes first. The point to be noted is that the growing India-China connectivity, say in the form of talks at the political level, can only help the two nations in understanding the perspectives of each other. Whether it can lead to a permanent settlement of the border issue is open to debate as each party may not be willing to make compromises on strategic aspects concerning territorial sovereignty.

Indian perspectives tend to project China as a country with territorial ambitions. Examples being quoted in India in this regard include Mao's description of China's 'palm' (Tibet) and 'five fingers' (Nepal, Sikkim, Bhutan, NEFA and Ladakh). References are also being made in India to the PRC's sense of 'historical loss' of territories expressed through their maps and atlas series, published in the eighties. Such maps had even been seen claiming that India's Assam, and even Andamans, were 'historically' parts of China.

China's claims are based on its historical stand – all its borders, including those with India, are as defined during the Qing dynasty period which ended in 1912. The root of the border problem with India lies in Beijing's position that a large chunk of its territory, especially the 90,000 sq km area in the Eastern sector, were illegally taken away by British India, after the 1914 Simla Convention and that India inherited the British legacy. This has provided the rationale for Beijing for rejecting the McMahon Line, a product of the Convention and in claiming the entire Arunachal Pradesh state of India as part of Chinese territory, referred to as 'Southern Tibet' by China. Authoritative scholars in China have categorically stated that Beijing cannot recognize the McMahon Line. If it did so, it would amount to Chinese admission of the 1962 conflict as a 'war of aggression' as well as an implicit acknowledgement that Tibet was once independent of China. On the other hand, for India, the McMahon Line remains its *de jure* border with China.

The current scenario firmly points to China's strategic thinking disallowing any compromise on the border issue. The Sino-Indian border talks, despite having completed thirteen rounds of talks between two special representatives, from the two sides, though useful in building confidence among the two sides, have not led to any tangible results towards finalising a 'framework' for a boundary settlement in accordance with the Agreement on Political Parameters, reached in 2005. While Beijing's stand is to approach the border issue in the spirit of 'mutual understanding and mutual accommodation', India wants 'ground realities' to be taken into account. About the reported Chinese claim over Tawang, an interesting argument is that besides strategic factors, the same has been due to China's fears that Buddhist monasteries in the border, including the one in Tawang, have been centres of Tibetan resistance to the Chinese authority and as such, should be taken over by it. Interestingly, the Chinese have introduced some new elements to the border question by questioning the already agreed position of keeping areas with settled populations out of the dispute. Is China ready for accommodation on the border issue? The statement made by the PRC Ambassador to India in November 2006, that both sides should make 'compromises' on the 'disputed' Arunachal Pradesh region, may be meaningful in this regard.

As indicators of China's tough stand on the border, it is of late claiming the 2.1 sq km 'finger point area' of Sikkim, the status of which as an Indian state has already been recognized by Beijing *de facto*. The reported Chinese intrusions, said to number 270 in 2008, into the Indian border, the adverse reaction of Beijing to the visit of the Indian Prime Minister Dr. Manmohan Singh to Arunachal Pradesh, China's bid to stop loans for Arunachal Pradesh from the Asian Development Bank, strong Chinese state-controlled media criticisms of India's dispatch of additional troops to the region, and positioning of advanced fighter aircraft on its eastern border and rise in the level of Chinese media rhetoric against India, noticed in 2009, need to be seen in the same light.

China's general stand is to 'shelve' difficult border issues like the one with India and instead work for 'common development'. For example the PRC wants to 'shelve' the South China Sea territorial dispute, leave the Senkaku issue with Japan for 'future generations' to solve and 'put aside the Sino-Indian border dispute waiting for a suitable climate for solution', (Deng Xiaoping to the then Indian leader Vajpayee, Beijing, 1979). What should be noted is that China never gives up its claims on sovereignty over disputed areas. An example is the Japan-China settlement on exploring the disputed Chunxiao gas field in the East China Sea. Though Beijing has agreed for joint development of the field, it has declared that China's sovereignty over the field is indisputable. A 'Draft Law on the Environment Protection of Sea Islands', which stipulates that 'ownership of the uninhabited islands shall revert to the state' and that 'the State Council of the People's Republic of China shall exercise control' over them, is under discussion in China's parliament. The Draft appears to include the Senkaku (Diaoyutai) Islands disputed between China and Japan in the East China Sea and Nansha (Spratly) Islands disputed between China and a number of countries including Malaysia, Philippines and Vietnam. China's 'shelving' formula, while it keeps territorial claims intact, may look suspicious to all neighbouiring countries having territorial disputes with China. As this writer views this situation, this formula has inherent flaws – for some at least, the projected completion of China's military modernization in 2050 may create new pressures on the leaders in Beijing at that time to become aggressive on all border issues. Especially for India and China, serious efforts are required to be made by them to find a 'compromise-based' solution to the border issue, sooner rather than later.

For the same strategic reasons, the India-China connectivity may not proceed further in contributing towards attending to other issues, viz. the Tibet issue, the China-Pakistan nexus, the PRC's defence modernization, China's policy towards India's neighbourhood, India-US relations and the East Asia integration process. On the first, it can be said that with India accepting the Tibet Autonomous Region as an integral part of China and standing firmly against any anti-China activity of the Dalai Lama from India's soil, this issue does not figure in Sino-Indian State-to-State relations. However, Beijing appears to be having reservations on India's motives with respect to the Dalai Lama. China's fears need to be understood in the context of the March 2008 unrest in Tibet, posing a challenge to China's sovereignty over that territory, even weakening Beijing's position in its border negotiations with India. Also, the question as to why India is tolerating the Tibetan Government in Exile on its soil, seems to be bothering China. Premier Wen Jiabao's description of the Tibet issue as a 'sensitive' one in relations with India, assumes significance in the context of what has been said above.

Chinese suspicions on India-Dalai Lama relations are not going to disappear soon. The picture may change if talks between Beijing and the exiled spiritual leader succeed, but chances in this regard appear to be bleak, at least for the moment. The China-Pakistan nexus is the next major bilateral issue. India-China connectivity has not led to any visible improvement on this account. A better understanding is required in China about India's sensitivities on this subject. Meanwhile, Chinese military, missiles and nuclear help to Pakistan continue. The latest example is China's plans to establish two civilian nuclear reactors in Pakistan, bypassing the stipulations of the Nuclear Suppliers Group mechanism. It is obvious that Beijing wants to ensure India-Pakistan nuclear balance.

India-China connectivity has also not been able to build confidence in India about the peaceful purposes of China's military modernization programme. China's policy is to mesh its 'peaceful development' and 'military modernisation' into one goal. It wants to create a 'prosperous country and strong army' (Fu Guo Qiang Jun). Chinese strategists explain that the PRC should utilize the peace time to prepare for war contingencies as well as to deter wars. China's assertiveness in the South China Sea and East China Sea, witnessed in recent times, indicates that its uncompromising stand on territorial issues would last forever. Outside China, it is therefore being realized that there is a mismatch between China's peaceful development goal and military modernization objective and that Beijing is displaying a deliberate ambiguity.

India's concerns over China's military modernization are being expressed through its important government documents, viz. the Defence Ministry's Annual Report (2008-2009) has said that the programme has implications for India's defence and security. Asking Beijing to show greater transparency in its defence policy and postures, particularly on the double-digit growth in defence spending in last two decades, it has observed that China's stated aim in its Defence White Paper for 2008 to develop missiles, space-based assets and blue water naval capabilities will have an effect on the overall military environment in the neighbourhood of India.

China, on its part, is alleging that India's defence strategy is visualizing war on two fronts – Pakistan and China. A Chinese comment (*China Youth Daily*) has said that India's real target is China, not Pakistan. India is especially viewing the ongoing momentum in building military infrastructure in Tibet, with concern.

India's concerns also relate to China's attempts to establish a strategic presence in India's neighbourhood viz. port projects like Gwadar (Pakistan), Hambantota (Sri Lanka), Chittagong (Bangladesh). They are giving rise to fears in India of a Chinese encirclement of the country, under what has come to be known as a 'string-of-pearls strategy'. The PRC has taken care to officially repudiate such concerns, by asserting that it has no plans to try for domination of the shipping lanes in the Indian Ocean and has no intention to establish a chain to encircle India.

Chinese critical positions on India-US relations are also complicating India-China ties. The Chinese have welcomed the India-US Strategic Dialogue and are themselves promoting ties with the US. Still, China seems to nurture fears of a US-India collusion against it. Its official media description recently of India's policy as one 'befriending the far and attacking the near', is unmistakably an indirect, but strong criticism of the developing strategic relations between India and the US.

It would also be necessary for China to pay attention to the Indian perception that it hesitates to accept India's leading role in the East Asian regional integration process on the plea that the process should only be based on ASEAN+3 (China, Japan and South Korea) cooperation, and that 'outsiders' like India, Australia and New Zealand, have no place in it.

The Indian public does not understand the reasons behind the appearance of hawkish views on India in some of China's strategic journals/websites. *Global Times* and writers like Colonel Dai Xu, have often given controversial views on India. How far such views reflect official thinking remains a question in India. Is the People's Liberation army (PLA) influencing China's foreign policy making? Even the US Defence Secretary Robert Gates has hinted at such possibilities (Shangrila Dialogue, Singapore, 2010). The answer to such misgivings may lie in the need for reporting transparency in China.

Both India and China can however immediately exploit the connectivity factor in addressing issues of a non-strategic nature, such as river water dispute, trade imbalance, unskilled Chinese labour in India, and import into India of Chinese telecom equipment.

In conclusion, it can be said that the existing India-China connectivity should not be overly hyped. Strategic issues dividing them are very deep and not going to disappear too soon. This will have implications for the region's stability and prosperity. Connectivity efforts should however continue, irrespective of their inherent limitations with respect to solving strategic issues. But solutions to dividing issues should come from within the two nations. As far as India is concerned, the nature of the issues demands it to be reactive to China's policies and China has therefore a greater responsibility in resolving them. Basically, much would depend upon the ability of the future leaderships in the two nations to effectively address the problems arising from their different strategic perceptions in a spirit of trust and mutual benefit. If this is not done, the strong expectations now on the 21st Century being an Asian Century with India and China playing pivotal roles may have little chances of becoming a reality.

5
The North-East in India's Look East: A Focus on Connectivity and Development in the Region

Soma Ghosal

The North-East of India has always been a region of considerable geo-strategic importance. Having common borders with Bangladesh, Bhutan, Nepal, Myanmar and China and close ethnic ties with the South East Asia, the region is witness to a confluence of tradition and modernity. While on the one hand, some of the 'revisionist local histories' have inspired the independentists,[1] on the other, the forces of globalization have reinforced the need for the region's proactive role in trans-border cultural and economic ties. The nature of international political boundaries in South Asia was a colonial legacy followed by the Partition that till date, has succeeded in sustaining stresses and strains amongst the neighbours. The duress of the North-East has to be understood in this historical perspective. The sensitivity of the region and increased concerns about national security have increasingly relegated its economic relevance to the background. The North-East of India came more into focus because of the various insurgency movements and protracted armed struggles that often sought independence from the Indian state.

The change came about in the 1990s, when with the initiation of India's Look East Policy, the economic importance of India's North-East saw resurgence. One of the early initiatives undertaken by India under its Look East Policy was the formation of a sub-regional grouping in 1997, called BIST-EC, comprising Bangladesh, India, Sri Lanka and Thailand. This later saw the addition of Myanmar, Bhutan and Nepal and was re-phrased BIMSTEC or the Bay of Bengal Initiative for Multi-Sectoral Technical and Economic Cooperation. BIMSTEC identified six areas of cooperation and stressed upon the establishment of economic links between India and the peninsula member countries of ASEAN, through the North-East of India. All the subsequent initiatives in India's Look East Policy, like the Mekong Ganga Cooperation (MGC) in 2000, which also includes Myanmar, Thailand, Laos, Cambodia and Vietnam, that came up with a set of guidelines known as the "Vientiane Declaration", and the Bangladesh-China-India-Myanmar Regional Economic Forum (BCIM) better known as the Kunming Initiative, have continued to emphasize the North-East as a vital link in the cross-border cultural interactions and economic development programmes. As the rapid growth of India started to make significant impact on the world economy, Indian policy-makers actively sought to strengthen India's global linkages and to accelerate its integration with the world economy. In this context, India's Look East Policy is a vital cog in this new geo-strategic configuration. As Prime Minister, Dr. Manmohan Singh had pointed out, the Look East Policy was not merely an external economic policy; it was also a strategic shift in India's vision of the world and India's place in the evolving global economy. International bodies like the IMF link the success of India in these globalizing efforts with her increasing role in the world economy.[2] It is in this era of globalism that the North-Eastern region of India has seen new opportunities that could 'enable it to get out of the territorial trap and relate to its trans-national neighbours on the east, culturally and economically.'[3] The global economic map today looks at 'region states' where the West's clichéd nomenclatures of dividing the world into distinct geographical regions are increasingly being challenged. It is thus that the idea of the geographical separation of South Asia and South East Asia is termed a fiction. As Baruah says, 'There are no 'natural' geographical boundaries separating South and South East Asia along the Indo-Myanmar border. In territorial terms, today's South Asia is, to a large extent, a successor to the entity called British India. North-East India's ties – historical, cultural, social, and economic – therefore do not stop at these international boundaries.[4] This is, perhaps, in the same vein as how B.G. Verghese had portrayed the North-East when he wrote, 'It is necessary to place it within a trans-border setting embracing a far wider geo-political region straddling the Eastern Himalayan-Patkai divide from the lower Ganga-Brahmaputra to the Mekong and Upper Yangtse basins.'[5]

The Focus on Connectivity

India launched its Look East Policy in 1991, yet, focus on the connectivity between her North-East and South East Asia assumed importance only with the induction of Myanmar as a full member of ASEAN in 1997. In order to make the Look East Policy relevant to the region, Indian policy makers have laid great emphasis on enhancing connectivity through all the possible modes of infrastructure development, such as land routes, railways, air connectivity, waterways, energy infrastructure development, both in the field of hydroelectric and hydrocarbon, and telecommunication linkages. In almost all the multilateral arrangements that India was a party to, the key areas of focus had been technology, transport and communication and energy, besides trade and investment, and tourism amongst others. Though India's Look East Policy encompasses a large volume of trade through the sea routes, yet the initiative does provide ample opportunities of developing the land routes through Myanmar to South East Asia and China. With Myanmar acting as a land bridge between the landlocked North-East and other regions of South East Asia, development in the region is being seen to receive a fillip. According to an official of the Ministry of External Affairs, the Look East Policy 'envisages the North-East region not as the periphery of India, but as the centre of a thriving and integrated economic space linking two dynamic regions with a network of highways, railways, pipelines, transmission lines crisscrossing the region.' In November 2004, while flagging off the ASEAN – India car rally in Guwahati,

Prime Minister, Dr. Manmohan Singh referred to India's North-East as a gateway to an "Asian Century".[6]

One of the early conscious efforts in boosting the connectivity of the region and facilitating cross-border trade came in the form of the Indo-Myanmar Trade Agreement signed on 31 January, 1994. The agreement specified that trade would be conducted on the basis of equality and mutual benefit through designated custom posts, viz., (a) Moreh in India (Manipur State) and Tamu in Myanmar, (b) Champhai in India (Mizoram State) and Hri in Myanmar and (c) other places that may be notified by mutual agreement between the two countries. The border trade at Moreh (India) and Tamu (Myanmar) was opened on 12th April, 1995. The agreement initially provided for cross-border trade in twenty two products, mostly agricultural/primary commodities produced in the trading countries. In 2001, a few more items were added to the list of tradable items. In practice, the agreement actually did not go much beyond according a formal sanction to exchanges traditionally going on between the local populations in the border areas of the two countries. However, the most notable development in this regard was the 165-km-long Indo-Myanmar Friendship Road connecting Tamu and Kalaymyo-Kalewa. In a highly publicised event in 2001, the then External Affairs Minister, Jaswant Singh, inaugurated the Tamu-Kalewa-Kalemyu road in Myanmar. The Rs. 90-crore road, built by India's Border Roads Organisation was India's gift to Myanmar.[7] The concept of an integrated check post at Moreh was a new concept aimed at managing both trade, cargo and passenger movement across the border and provide modern infrastructure facilities and better connectivity. The objective was to facilitate regional trade and also help local communities living in the vicinity of border towns through which the trade took place. The Construction Minister of Myanmar, Major-General Saw Tun felt the road would be a vital link in the Asian Highway project connecting Singapore to Istanbul and passing through Myanmar and India.[8] The technical and funding issues of the transnational highway were discussed at a meeting between the Foreign Ministers of Myanmar, Thailand and India, in Delhi, in December 2003. Another of such hyped connectivity projects is the Kaladan Multi-Modal Transit Transport Facility aimed at establishing connectivity between Indian ports on the eastern side and Sittwe port in Myanmar, through a riverine transport corridor with the road in Mizoram envisaged as an alternative trade route to the North-East.[9] For the purposes of Burmese gas transfer through the North-East, India's investment plan of $100 million aims at improving the old colonial port of Sittwe on the west coast of Myanmar.[10]

Colonial Legacy

The question of connectivity between India and South East Asia through the North-East had always been a vital one during the colonial period. A glance at any of the up and coming projects would reveal that most of the road links were a colonial legacy and their disruption was, also, one of the blatant negative aspects of the colonial policy of destroying all trans-border economic and cultural ties. The initial British policy of improving connectivity in the region stemmed from the twin needs of securing the eastern frontier of India by subduing the wild tribes of the North-East and simultaneously keeping the ambitious designs of the kingdom of Burma in check. The British later embarked on a mission to develop a shorter land route to China and explore opportunities in developing the road connectivity with the southeastern region, and further north. The Second World War further impressed upon the British the need to develop roads for evacuating British citizens from Burma and for creating a supply route for the army when the Japanese attacked Burma. The British project of construction of motorable roads took shape with the aid of the Indian Tea Association (ITA) and materialized into three roads across the Patkai. These were the Tamu – Imphal – Dimapur Road, the Imphal – Bishenpur – Silchar Road and the routes in the extreme North-East, via the Hukawng Valley and the Patkai mountains to Ledo and thence by train or steamer down to the Brahmaputra Valley. These roads were necessary for carrying supplies to the army and the civil administration and responsible for getting as many refugees to safety as possible. The project of road making by the British India government and the Indian Tea Association began in early March 1942, and by early May, these roads were ready for a limited amount of motorable traffic and an unlimited number of refugees on foot. However, in many places these roads were a little more than a track and were rendered incommunicable during the monsoons. In May 1942, when Mandalay and Myitkina fell to the

Japanese the need for alternative communication routes became imperative. It was, then, that evacuation was planned through the Hukawng Valley and over the Pangsau Pass, at a height of more than 4,000 feet. The road on both sides of the Pass was a little more than a mule track. There was a descent of about 900 feet on the Assam side into the Naga village of Nongki. From Nongki one could reach Nampong and then on to Lekhapani, the base camp on the Indian side. The track was a difficult one, marked by undulating terrain, rivers with strong currents, dense vegetation, steep slopes and frequent landslides and deep gorges.[11]

The Stilwell Road

The Kunming Initiative, born out of the Conference at Kunming, the capital of the Yunnan province of China, in August 1999, was the outcome of the desire of the four participating members, Bangladesh, India, Myanmar and China towards facilitating trade between them and the development of regional resources. The reconstruction of the 'Burma Road' was one of the main projects under this initiative. The revival of the ancient Burmese trade route linking south-west China with the Indian subcontinent through Myanmar was seen as a key connectivity project in the trans-region economic development. The construction of the famous Stilwell Road, a road named after an American general who oversaw its construction at the height of World War II, also known as the Burma Road, connecting Dimapur, Kohima and Imphal to Burmese towns, was an engineering marvel in any period of history. The Stillwell Road was initially termed 'an impossible engineering pipe dream'. Nevertheless, the road was completed in two and a half years. The first truck on this road rumbled across in October 1944. For the next sixteen months numerous convoys passed through portions of this road but the first overland vehicle convoy from India to Kunming in China began from Ledo in January 1945, and the lead truck carried banners that read: First Convoy Ledo Road. However, the importance of the road was short lived as the war with Burma ended on 4 August, 1945. Thereafter, this famous road fell silent and was written off as a no-man's land.[12] This strategic road network provided a base for future economic and cultural cooperation between India's North-East and South East Asia – an unintended legacy of the war. Old official documents refer enthusiastically to the Delhi-Chungking Road as Kunming was connected by road to the city (now spelt Chongqing) that was the virtual capital of China during World War II. Events, however, took a different turn with an inward looking Burma and conflicts in South East Asia.[13]

The 1,736-kilometre Stilwell Road, once re-opened, will link North-Eastern India not just with Yunnan but with other parts of China and South East Asia as well as other roads that were branching out from the Stilwell Road that provided connectivity with Thailand, Cambodia and Vietnam. Such connectivity would not only expedite the transit of goods, but also cut down costs as pointed out by Pradyut Bordoloi, Assam's Commerce and Industries Minister and an ardent advocate of reopening the road. According to him, if the goods went via the Stilwell Road, they would reach Yunnan in two days and would reduce transport costs by more than 30 per cent.[14] About 61 km of the Stilwell Road runs through India, 1,033 km through Myanmar and 632 km into China. Interestingly, China has converted the 620 km Stilwell Road passing through its territories into a multi-lane international highway. It has also earmarked $2.5 billion to develop cross-border roads in Myanmar, stretching for about 1,033 km. The 61-km stretch of the same road on the Indian side is yet to be reconstructed, though lobbying for reopening the road has been on for some time. Former Minister of State for Commerce, Jairam Ramesh had once said that he would like to see the road reopened by 2010. Then a June 18, 2009, report from Guwahati, quoting B.K. Handique, Minister for Development of North-Eastern Region, said that plans to reopen had been shelved following Myanmar's objection on security grounds. Setong Sena, Finance Minister of Arunachal Pradesh, had been among those who had visited the Prime Minister's Office to seek the reopening of the Stilwell Road. According to him, the government had put the Stilwell Road as a third priority after routes had opened in Mizoram and Manipur.[15]

When connectivity is the buzz word behind all the trans-border trade and investment activities in the region, certain ground realities cannot be ignored. In India's Look East Policy, the China factor is a key player, yet the hard statistics are difficult to ignore. During 1997-98 and 2006-07, in percentage terms, trade between ASEAN and India had grown slowly, from 7.68 per cent to 10.08 per cent. In 2005-06, India's total exports were about $10.4 billion, while her imports were $10.88 billion. In 1991, China-ASEAN trade was only about $8 billion. In 2005, it touched the $130.4 billion mark, registering a 15-fold increase. China and ASEAN are now the fourth biggest trading partners of each other. ASEAN is China's fourth biggest export market and the third biggest source of import. By the end of June 2006, ASEAN had made a total net investment of $40 billion in China. There was a corresponding growth of Chinese investment in ASEAN, which was also becoming an attractive investment destination for Chinese companies and vice-versa.[16] But with the case of India and ASEAN, such complementarities do not exist as both seek entry into the EU and US markets to expand their share in exports. Indo-ASEAN trade has developed, however, indirectly, as after 'liberalisation', several foreign and Indian firms procure their spare equipment from their bases in ASEAN countries, especially in computers, electronics and chemicals. The North-East as a part of this process is yet in a formative stage. The volume of border trade with Myanmar, especially, under the 1994 Indo-Myanmar agreement, has yet to gain momentum. India's exports to Myanmar in 2005-06 of top 20 commodities was worth $110.7 million, while the imported commodities were worth about $526 million – a modest volume by any standard.[17] However, there are signs of optimism. In July 2007, the then Union Minister of State for Commerce, Jairam Ramesh, while addressing visiting journalists from the Association of South East Asian Nations, had said that India was looking at developing its border areas with the group, into a growth triangle. Ramesh had listed the natural resources of the North-East, namely gas, coal and hydro power which, he said, had not been tapped. India's North-East, nestled at the foothills of the Himalayas, was extremely rich in biodiversity and boasted of a wide variety of spices, medicinal and aromatic herbs and a range of fruits and flowers that were yet to find their way to the malls of India and the world.[18]

Connectivity, Peace and Development in the North-East

In one of his memorial lectures, B.G. Verghese had pondered upon the inextricable bond between peace, development and connectivity in the North-East. Some decision makers in Delhi, he said, feared that the opening up of the region externally could invite trouble, giving a fillip to attempts at destabilizing the region and result in the dumping of goods in this sensitive region. But to the contrary, he felt that opening up through Bangladesh and Myanmar to the wider neighbourhood beyond, along with appropriate trade facilitation measures could help legitimize commerce, expand income generation and employment opportunities, promote tourism and create an enabling environment conducive to peace and stability. Remote boundaries at the edges of what had hitherto been peripheral regions, Verghese felt, had to be seen as gateways and not barriers and India should open up the lifelines to integrate the North-East which was ready for the move.[19]

Though the Look East Policy of India presupposes that heightened trade relations and free markets with South East Asia would lift the North-East out of the shackles of insurgency, poverty, and economic backwardness, yet the skepticism continues. In fact, in one of his speeches to an audience in the North-East, Pranab Mukherjee had admitted that though the Look East Policy was enormously beneficial to India at large, it was creating fears amongst the local people of being submerged by the grand Indian vision of 'opening up' to South East Asia and flooding a fragile region with the logic of market economics. He stated, "I am aware that many fear that accelerated cooperation could in fact pose serious challenges. These concerns or challenges need to be listed out; we need to dwell on how they may be addressed.... there is considerable urgency in this." Jairam Ramesh, another strong supporter of opening up of borders in the eastern sector, had also voiced his concerns regarding the connectivity through Myanmar. "If there is cross-border terrorism in relation to Jammu and Kashmir, it is happening in Nagaland and Manipur also. In relation to AIDS, it is a different form of cross-border terrorism. We cannot turn a blind eye towards the regional dimensions of this issue...."[20]

Problems and Prospects

The problems for India, notwithstanding, China, too, had its own share of problems. The Yunnan province is very much a mirror image of India's North-East, a cradle for potential secessionist movements. Yunnan's population, in Chinese official parlance, is made up of 26 ethnic nationalities, quite similar to the presence of myriad tribes in India's North-East. Though China has been following a policy of official support for the cultural revival of its ethnic minorities, scholars like Edward Friedman, Eric Mueggler and others see the cultural resurgence as a kind of 'exit' strategy by which minorities reconstitute a collective identity and existence outside the Han-centric mainstream. Mueggler, for example, argues that the re-emergence of traditional practices in the Yi community in northern Yunnan is bound up with the criticism of the state, its grand schemes and efforts to assert control. Mette Hansen has also pointed out such undercurrents of anti-establishment amongst the Dai minority nationality, the third largest minority nationality in Yunnan.[21] The fear of separatist movements from the minorities is omnipresent in China's minorities' policy and there have been repeated warnings from the leadership of crushing such ethnic unrest with a heavy hand. However, China has sought to consolidate and expand elements of minority identity and practice with its promotion of political and economic goals. It has thus set up an International Regional Cooperation Office in Yunnan to focus on a very clear development strategy for the province which is set to become another economic hub. The packaging of minority traditions in the province is also in consonance with this purpose of economic development. Besides, China has diligently pursued the modernisation of its infrastructure, while India has a long way to go. The state of roadways all across the North-East of India is in a pathetic condition and most of the road connectivity to towns and villages get completely cut off during the monsoons. Even the roads to Moreh and Champhai, significant border towns with potential for a heightened border trade, remain in an abysmal condition. One of the major impediments in developing the sector is that the North-East is an insurgency-afflicted region and there are constant fears that the road connectivity would facilitate movement of insurgents, arms and drugs. The Indo-Myanmar border has traditionally been an illicit drug producing area. All the border towns on the connectivity routes, including Moreh and Champhai and the Pangsau Pass, fall on the route for illicit trafficking of drugs, mainly heroin, into India and the smuggling of ephedrine into Myanmar. The drug routes are not just restricted to the Indo-Myanmar border alone. One of the principal pipelines of the heroin trail leaves Myanmar and passes through China's Yunnan province and then go on to Hong Kong or the free-trade zones around Guangdong.[22] Other problems go hand in hand. Attempts at legitimizing the border trade along the Indo-Myanmar border, have witnessed a parallel trade in contraband. One singular instance of this is that while the old Stilwell Road is still used by local traders, a significantly greater business has involved the illegal trafficking between India, China, Myanmar and South East Asia. A reopening would convert much of this contraband trade to legitimate business.

The insurgency situation along the proposed routes to the gateways of the trans-Asian cooperation like the Asian

Highway is another area of concern. The United National Liberation Front of Manipur (UNLF) operates mostly from the hilly areas of Myanmar, bordering Moreh. The outfit crosses the Indo-Myanmar border with impunity and creates violence in these areas. There also exists a Kuki National Liberation Front (KNLF) spearheaded by the Kuki National Army (KNA), which dominates Moreh and the route en-route to Moreh. Despite signing a Suspension of Operations (SOO) with the Indian Army, the KNLF and the KNA openly extort huge amounts of money from the local traders on NH-39, generic to border trade. This can be blatantly witnessed by any casual tourist to the area travelling with the local traders. Myanmar, too, is beset with its own problems of insurgency. Myanmar maintains that the Stilwell Road passes through its Kachin region and is infested with militant camps belonging to the outfits from India's North-East and the reopening of the road would provide better access to the rebels. The Kachin region in the north Sagaing division of Myanmar is said to be home to about eight rebel groups of India's North-East, including the S.S. Khaplang faction of the National Socialist Council of Nagaland (NSCN–K) and the United Liberation Front of Asom (ULFA). There has always been a close cooperation between the Kachin rebel outfits and the Naga rebels especially of the Khaplang group. The tribal unrest in neighbouring Burma had long served as an inspiration to the sub-nationalist movements across the border.

It is, thus, not without reason that India's border with

Myanmar is often thought of as a dead end to trade, porous only to militants and drug traffickers. The long-running insurgencies along India's North-Eastern border, the confused political situation in Myanmar, and a somewhat short-sighted policy in New Delhi in dealing with these issues, have acted as a spanner to the much-touted objectives of the Look East Policy in the region. But, things might be beginning to change. There is, today, a virtual boom in the construction of cross-national highways, road, rail and air corridors, thanks to the interest of multilateral organizations and advanced industrial countries with a stake in the globalized economy. Multilateral initiatives have brought together donor countries, land-locked developing countries and transit developing countries on infrastructure development, trade facilitation and regional cooperation projects in many parts of the world. But when it comes to building roads through Myanmar, multilateral development assistance has been unavailable because of the economic sanctions imposed by the US and the European Union. India too, had a critical stance towards Myanmar's military rulers, in the years following their violent crackdown of the democracy movement in 1988. But there was a U-turn in Indian policies in 1993, brought about by the concern over the economic, political and military inroads made by China in the intervening period in the state.[23]

Today China, India and Thailand, provide bilateral assistance to Myanmar. There is also a growing realization in the West that sanctions against Myanmar are not working.

Any tangible solution to the problems of insurgency, drugs and arms trafficking in the region can be achieved through the arena of bilateral and multilateral cooperation as none of these problems can be viewed in isolation. Connectivity, especially through a highly effective road and rail system through the landlocked region, is being seen as a vital remedy to several of these maladies. As the former Director-General of the Border Security Force, E.N. Rammohan, had pointed out in an essay in 2005, "Roads are the first enemies of insurgents. Denied of a hinterland, he has no place to retreat. Today this is the first step to be taken by the government of India."[24] This is corroborated by studies on the illicit drug producing areas of the Golden Crescent across Pakistan and Afghanistan where poppy cultivation goes unabated due to the relative inaccessibility of some of these regions that enjoy a semi-autonomous status. There have been attempts to build roads through the Shin Qamar region, 50 kms west of the NWFP capital, which have been violently resisted.

In the small town of Moreh in Manipur, where the National Highway 39 hits the border, work has begun on the truly ambitious border infrastructure. This is the Indian link-up with a refurbished NH-39 that would eventually become a part of a long dreamed-of trans-Asian road system. Of course, ambitious attempts to integrate the North-East have been begun before. It was thought at one point in time that Myanmar was willing to upgrade the old Stilwell Road that linked it to India, and in the process helping to connect the North-East to a usable port. That, along with similar hopes from an improvement in Indo-Bangladesh relations, has not exactly come to fruition yet. But India cannot afford to sit back and let its neighbours dictate the pace of this process. If the infrastructure gets built, the incentives for them to do their part will become ever clearer. There is already considerable optimism amongst the local business community across both sides of the border. Myanmar's traders and officials at Tamu town, now, are seeking an improvement in Manipur's law and order situation so that border trade with India could be enhanced. This is definitely a positive signal from the reticent neighbour. In 2007, the Cabinet Committee on Economic Affairs (CCEA) approved the expansion of the Special Accelerated Road Development Programme (SARDP) for the North-East that sought to expedite the construction of the Stilwell Road.[25] In March, this year, the Indian Chamber of Commerce, Kolkata, had organized the 'Look East Summit 2010'. The summit focused on pursuing the 2Cs – commerce and connectivity – and deliberated upon the prospects of trade and investment in South East Asia along with regional integration and the scope for enhancing foreign trade and connectivity between India and the ASEAN countries. This was a significant event in that it was attended by the Ambassadors of Laos, Thailand, Indonesia and Myanmar. What assumed importance was the inaugural speech of the Governor of Arunachal Pradesh, J.J. Singh, wherein he emphasized the importance of road connectivity, especially, on developing the historic Stilwell Road. The road, he felt, would offer considerable distance advantage over the existing Mandalay highway and would be extremely beneficial to the region enabling the revival of formal border trade from the Pangsau Pass in Changlang district as also reviving the local industries in Assam and Arunachal Pradesh.[26] Many analysts also feel that once the border trade is allowed to take place in a transparent and orderly manner, many dynamic economic forces would be unleashed on both sides of the border, leading to opening up of mutually beneficial areas of economic cooperation. The Asian Development Bank has viewed investment in connectivity as an effective tool in poverty reduction and income generation. By linking poor, remote villages to markets, such roads can help reduce non-income poverty through access to health and education services. Connectivity projects, it feels, are best when they are cognizant of social and environmental issues and provide for shared resource management in an integrated way.[27] There is ample scope for the North-East, if viewed in this light, and the dreams can turn to reality if there is a positive approach both within the region and among the policy makers at the helm.

Notes and References

1. Sanjib, Baruah, *Durable Disorder: Understanding the Politics of Northeast India*, New Delhi, OUP, 2005, p. 215.
2. T.N., Srinivasan, 'China, India and the World Economy,' *Economic and Political Weekly*, Aug. 26-Sept. 1, 2006, p. 3718.
3. Sanjib, Baruah, op. cit., p. 217.
4. Ibid., p. 215.

5. B.G., Verghese, *India's North-East Resurgent: Ethnicity, Insurgency, Governance, Development*, New Delhi, Konark Publishers Ltd., 1996, Preface.
6. *The Statesman*, March 16, 2009.
7. Sanjib, Baruah, op. cit., p. 224.
8. Ibid.
9. *The Financial Express*, April 4, 2008.
10. Ibid.
11. Sukanya, Sharma, 'Building Roads to Myanmar: A Historical Overview,' *Economic and Political Weekly*, Nov. 26-Dec. 2, 2005, p. 5127.
12. Mamang, Dai, '*Butterflies over the Stilwell Road*,' Internet Edition, Feb. 3, 2009.
13. *The Statesman*, Jun 1, 2009.
14. Sudha, Ramachandran, 'The Road to Riches – Asian Highway,' *Asia Times*, Oct. 19, 2008.
15. *The Hindu*, May 2, 2010.
16. *The Statesman*, July 16 2007.
17. Ibid., June 1, 2009.
18. *The Statesman*, July 16, 2007.
19. B.G., Verghese, 'Northeast: Unfinished Business. Pointers towards Restructuring, Reform, Reconciliation and Resurgence,' Internet article, can be accessed at www.bgverghese.com/northeast.htm accessed on Oct. 1, 2010.
20. *The Statesman*, March 19, 2007.
21. Nguyen Thi, Dieu, 'The State versus the Indigenous Peoples: The Impact of Hydraulic Projects on Indigenous Peoples of Asia,' *Journal of World History*, Vol. 7, No. 3, 1996. Also, Susan, McCarthy, 'Gods of Wealth, Temples of Prosperity: Party-State Participation in the Minority Cultural Revival', in *China: An International Journal*, Vol. 2, No. 1, 2004.

22. Matthew, Brzezinski, 'Re-engineering the Drug Business', *The New York Times*, June 23, 2002.
23. Sanjib, Baruah, 'Fresh Hope Rises in the East,' *The Telegraph*, Feb. 9, 2004.
24. *The Statesman*, March 19, 2007.
25. *The Indian Express*, Oct. 3, 2007.
26. *Arunachal News*, March 28, 2010.
27. Sukanya, Sharma, 'Building Roads to Myanmar: A Historical Overview', op. cit. p. 5128.

6
Do We Need to Reopen the Stilwell Road?

Lt. Gen. J.R. Mukherjee (Retd.)

The Ledo Road, was intended to be the primary all weather low altitude supply route to China during World War II, and was built under the direction of General Stilwell of the U.S. Army from the railhead at Ledo (Assam, India) across the Patkai Range through the Pangsau Pass (3,727 feet), through Burma towns of Shingbwiyang, Myitkyina and Bhamo in Kachin state to Mong-Yu road junction (748 kms from Ledo), where it joined the Burma Road so that supplies could be delivered to Kunming, Yunnan, starting in 1942. It was renamed the Stilwell Road after General Stilwell. The road was built by 15,000 American soldiers and 35,000 local workers at a cost of US$150 Million. In late 1944, it became a highway stretching from Assam, India to Kunming, China 1,079 miles (1,736 km) in length. The Stilwell Road on the Indian side is about 61 km long. The major stretch of 1,033 km lies within Myanmar, while the stretch in China is 632 km.

After Burma was liberated, the road gradually fell into disrepair. The last recorded vehicular journey over part of the road was by the veterans of the Burma Star Association in mid-2005 who were invited to join a 'down memory lane' trip to Shingbwiyang, organized by a politically well-connected travel agent and which successfully travelled the road. For many years, travel into the region was restricted because of an active insurgency against the Governments of India and Myanmar. With the improvement in relations between India and Myanmar, tourism has begun near Pangsau Pass. The road is still not fit for vehicular traffic – particularly in the Kachin belt and in many stretches where it is open, it is only single lane and fits only for 4 wheeled drive.

There are now increasing demands around the region to reopen the Stilwell Road as it would offer an excellent opportunity to Assam and Arunachal Pradesh to get connected to the economically flourishing parts of Yunnan and Southeast Asia via Myanmar and provide an additional land link for the growing economies of India and China. It is felt that this would also facilitate India's Look East Policy and greatly assist in rapid development of India's North-East. This road could easily handle a substantial part of India's growing bilateral trade with China because of cost and time benefits, and both sides would save much in transport costs in exporting and importing goods meant for India's eastern and North-Eastern regions and China's remote southwest. This road if renovated, would be capable of handling between 15 per cent and 20 per cent of the

Sino-Indian bilateral trade and would encourage Indian industry to invest in production hubs in India's under-developed North-Eastern states to make goods meant for export to China.

Today, the India's North-East region is being viewed with optimism as it is endowed with a gamut of untapped resources including large deposits of crude oil, petroleum products and natural gas, coal, minerals, cement, tea and fresh fruits which can be exported. It also produces good quality Era, Muga and also mulberry varieties of silk handicrafts and handlooms all of which are in great demand in the global market. If the hydro electric potential is utilized effectively, the region can export this resource to its trans-national trade partners. Economic integration with Southeast Asia and its neighbours offers enormous growth potential for North-East. It also has tremendous potential for tourism. Out of the North-East States, Assam enjoys geo-strategic positioning in the Northeast for boosting the volume of border trade with South East Asia and China.

Today, about a quarter of India's foreign trade comes from its Asian neighbours. A need is now being felt to shift the focus of the Look East Policy to India's North-East and work towards the revival of several strategic initiatives of the past including the Bay of Bengal Initiative for Multi-Sectoral Technical and Economic Cooperation (BIMSTEC) comprising Bangladesh, India, Sri Lanka, Myanmar, and Thailand, Mekong Ganga Cooperation (MGC) which includes India, Myanmar, Thailand, Laos, Cambodia and

Vietnam; Bangladesh-China-India-Myanmar Regional Economic Forum (BCIM); and the Kunming Initiative which provides an opportunity for India's North-East and Bangladesh to be integrated to trade with Myanmar and China.

But beyond border trade, Stilwell Road has emerged a serious contender as the eastern Indian entry point for the ambitious Asian Highway Network. A cooperative project among countries in Asia and the United Nations Economic and Social Commission for Asia and the Pacific (ESCAP) to improve the highway systems in Asia, it was initiated by the UN back in 1959 but stalled when finances and local geopolitics went sour in 1975. The eastern Indian entry is currently planned at the Moreh/Tamu in Manipur, which has limited border trade, thanks to 1995 agreement between India and Myanmar. Manipur also has the problem of being the most troubled state in India due to tremendous inter ethnic tension, strife, insurgency by both the Nagas and the Meiteis and all forms of smuggling and drug trafficking. The Stilwell Road has therefore become increasingly attractive for vastly shorter distances (openly championed by China and Thailand).

Of the three countries through which the Stilwell Road runs, Myanmar has so far not agreed to renovate and reopen the road. Without its consent, the plan to link Ledo with Kunming by road is futile. Unfortunately, it is Myanmar that has resisted the reopening of the Stilwell Road the most. This is partly because of the military junta's traditional wariness of opening the country to outsiders. Besides, the road runs through territory controlled by Kachin rebels. The 300 km stretch of the road passing through the Kachin area of Myanmar is home to many insurgent groups operating in the North-East. Considering the situation in Kachin state, where the junta has little control, and is in the process of launching military operations against them, Myanmar is not keen to reopen the road.

China on the other hand has pursued the idea of reopening the Stilwell Road with diligence. It has gone about repairing and reconstructing its stretch of the road and has already transformed this into a modern six-lane expressway. Chinese officials have also been persistent in their lobbying with officials in India and Myanmar to get them to repair the road and open it up for trade. China is also involved in the development of various segments of the Stilwell Road in Myanmar too. A 100 km stretch from Tengchong in Yunnan to the Warshoung in Kachin state of Myanmar was completed in April 2007. Another 224 km segment from Myitkyina in Kachin to Tengchong was completed in 2008. China is also assisting the rebuilding of a stretch of the Stilwell Road between Danai to Myitkyina in Kachin State of Myanmar. Thailand is also interested in the reopening of the Stilwell Road and has appealed to New Delhi to reopen this road.

Notwithstanding the romanticism involved in articulating the need to specifically reopen only the Stilwell Road and other issues above, are that a more rational stand that could be taken is that India and her North-East need to be opened up eastwards for trade – not necessarily only via the Stilwell Road, but along any viable route which would be discussed subsequently, should it be found that this route was not a viable option.

An opinion widely articulated across the North-East, whilst not so stated by the Government of India, is that India is also not in favour of reopening the Stilwell Road due to security concerns some of which are as follows:

- The North-East is an insurgency racked region and there are fears that the road would facilitate movement of insurgents, arms and drugs as happened, after the opening of India-Myanmar border at Moreh.
- The Indian government still does not enjoy very good relations with the military dictatorship in Myanmar primarily on account of the lack of democracy in Myanmar and the decade-long incarceration of the popularly elected leader Aung San Suu Kyi.
- The Chinese have been aggressively taking over trade in Myanmar. If the Stillwell Road is re-opened, they may take over the markets in the North-Eastern region of India turn them into dumping grounds for cheap Chinese goods, thereby undermining the local economy.
- India can also not forgive the Chinese for the 1962 war or ignore their regular intrusions in the North-Eastern region.

- There is also the issue of China's total support to Pakistan in their proxy war against India, nuclear proliferation and nuclear aid to Pakistan, direct support to India's North-East insurgents, and China's anti India Global Foreign Policy.
- The Chinese may also increase their influence over the people in the region.
- The terrain is so mountainous and hostile that road construction is expensive – some feel it is so expensive that it does not make sense in terms of economic returns to revive the Stillwell Road (Road Cost ₹ 3000 Cr to ₹ 4000 Cr for the 400 km stretch to link up the road to Myitkina).
- There is also concern that Northern Myanmar is now almost totally controlled by China. They are developing extensive infrastructural facilities from Yunnan through Northern Myanmar (rail, road, airports, sea ports and pipelines) which could easily be used by them for military purposes against India – this could develop into a new front which would need to be defended on the land, sea and air –in event of war between India and China. This can be ill afforded by India, whose armed forces are already hard pressed and over extended.

Those in favour of opening the road articulate that in addition to the benefits touched on earlier, it must be understood that:

- The North-East has 4,750 kms worth of international borders on almost all sides of the region with only a narrow area about 25 to 50 kms wide linking it to the rest of India through the Siliguri Corridor. North-Eastern states of India are closer to Yangon, Bangkok and some Chinese cities than New Delhi or Mumbai and thus offer better/cheaper trade options including basic daily necessities.
- Security concerns make it important to engage the resource rich region of south East Asian nations where China has already established a strong foothold. Reopening such communications to facilitate this engagement would help in the achievement of economic goals and good neighbourly relations. This would also counter China's degree of involvement in Southeast Asia.
- There is a need for India, China, Myanmar and South East Asian nations to cooperate extensively for economic gains – this demands creation of the necessary infrastructure to support the same.
- There have been several problems which have hampered development of India's North-East which have led to allegations by certain elements to exploit the situation by alleging 'alienation', 'exploitation' and 'insecurity', to initiate or prolong insurgency. This has meant political and economic instability so crucial for any meaningful development. The development initiatives under the 'Special Category Status', by the

Indian Government releasing large sums of money as development funds without creating necessary credit absorption capacity in the economy has hence largely not met with the desired results. Analysis indicates that if the border is opened up for overland trade with neighbouring countries, the North-East region would benefit economically immensely and that this would assist tremendously in its development.

- Unemployment in the North-East is one of its major problems which is aggravated by the isolation of the region. If the region can become the gateway of India to the East and, an economic hub between the rest of India and South East Asia/China a lot of employment could be generated.
- Yunnan is naturally interested in reviving links with the North-East as that will provide direct access to Indian and Western markets, which would otherwise involve a 7,000-km detour around Singapore.
- Myanmar and Bangladesh would also gain from the economic benefits of such trade.
- India needs to realize that the Chinese and the Burmese will always be India's neighbours – she therefore has to befriend and deal with them. Further, people on both sides of the border have close cultural and commercial links. Not formalizing these links commerce has only led to large scale smuggling.

- It is also possible for India to flood Chinese markets with Indian goods. Fears of possible economic domination by China are therefore exaggerated.
- It is imperative to put a road through to Yunnan – it would be seen subsequently that the cost of doing so need not be very high. Yunnan is already importing over half a million tonnes of iron ore from India annually, and exporting to it about a million tonnes of phosphatic ore – all this besides many other items. Substantial goods traffic is therefore already available to sustain this link. All this could easily be transported by road routes at a much lower cost.
- Opening such roads would also improve the tourism potential of the region.

In the overall strategic context therefore what are the options available to create better connectivity in the region and facilitate development of the North-East?

- The first option is to reconstruct the Stilwell Road from Ledo in Assam to Myitkina (about 400 kms) in Myanmar as discussed above linking upto the Chinese alignment to Kunming. This would provide the shortest route to Kunming along the new Chinese realignments – about 1450 kms from Ledo to Kunming. The new Chine alignments are however reported to have suffered damage due to this years' earthquakes and are now under renovation.

- The second possibility is to extend the Indian road from Moreh (Manipur) to Tamu further to Kalewa on the Chindwin River. If this river is bridged, a link would be established with Mandalay which is on the railway system of Myanmar with linkages onto the new road to Kunming. This is a better link to Southeast Asia.
- The third option is that Mizoram could be connected to the Myanmar port of Sitwe thus providing them access to the Bay of Bengal and also the Kunming – Sitwe corridor. This is already under development by China and will have road, rail and pipeline links from Sitwe to Kunming. This is being done by them to improve the lot of the interior backward regions of China which are currently facing social unrest due to uneven development. This corridor would also tremendously reduce costs on transportation of oil from the Middle East and Myanmar's offshore oilfields, as it would avoid tankers having to go through the pirate infested Mallacca Straits to Chinese ports and then to the interiors. It needs to be noted that China is putting in tremendous efforts to eradicate unrest by developing isolated regions such as Yunnan – India has much to learn from this. To this end it is also trying to improve the Myanmar railway system and the inland waterway of the Irrawaddy and routes to the rest of South East Asia to facilitate better trading infrastructure.

- Alternatively, the existing trade crossings between Myanmar and Mizoram via Champhai to Zowkhathar into Myanmar could be further developed to link up with option 2 above. The roads here are again already developed.

- The fourth option is that Agartala (Tripura) could be linked to the port of Chittagong (Bangladesh) with the consent of Bangladesh thereby giving Tripura and South Assam access to the sea.

- The fifth option is to utilize the little known but good National Highway from Upper Assam, i.e., Dibrugarh – Tinsukia – Chowkham – Tezu – Brahmakund Bridge- along the Lohit River to Hayuliang – Walong – Kibithu – Chinese Border at Kahao/Dichu (1400m and is open throughout the year) (Tezu to Dichu is about 234 kms) – On the Chinese (Tibet) side to Rima (Zayu) (about 50 kms from Dichu) along Highway S201 and G31B – Jidaxiang – Baxoi-linking on to the Chinese Eastern Highway (G214) going to Lhasa at Mangkang (about 650 kms). Till 1952 there was a Tibetan Trade Agent posted in Tezu (before 1950 at Sadiya) and an Indian one in Rima (Zayu as it is now called at 2,325 m). From this road junction the options are to go along the Eastern Highway to Lhasa, or along the super highways to the industrial town of Chengdu or along the Yunnan super highway to Kunming. This route offers the best direct option into China and is through except for a small patch to connect up at the border – the defence of this region is also adequately catered for. It is however more difficult as large tracts of it pass through high altitude terrain and it is longer than the Stilwell Road to reach Kunming.

When considered rationally, in the ultimate analysis I am personally of the view that all these roads are of great strategic, economic and developmental importance. We have tried the use of force now for a large number of years to try and quell social unrest and insurgency – used alone it has so far only been partially successful. It is therefore imperative that we give development a chance whilst simultaneously taking adequate measures in the realm of counter insurgency and other operations/measures to safeguard our security. It would hence be politically and economically beneficial to carry forward all these projects progressively and link them to the Trans Asian Highway system irrespective of the views of the 'Hawks' on the matter.

7
The Stillwell Road and India's Look East Policy

E.N. Rammohan

Introduction

"An immense laborious task, unlikely to be finished until the need for it had passed," was Sir Winston Churchill's terse appraisal of the controversial Ledo-Burma Road Project. Begun in 1942, by US Army Engineers, the project seemed an impossibility from the start. First, the stretch of the old Burma war-torn road leading east 600 miles from Mong Yu in North Burma to Kunming in China would have to be repaired and improved for all-weather travel. Then a new 500-mile road would have to be carved out of the wilderness from Ledo in Assam to Mong Yu. Eighty percent of the region through which the engineers had to cut their way was in enemy hands. As work on the road progressed, bulldozers frequently carried a man riding shotgun to guard against snipers, nevertheless some 139 engineers were killed by the Japanese. Diseases, drownings, crashes of supply planes and construction accidents claimed the lives of hundreds more. It was said without exaggeration that the road was being built at the cost of a man a mile. All told, 28,000 engineers and 35,000 native workers laboured for two years to complete the Ledo-Burma Road, known officially as the Stillwell Road. The road's construction – along the edges of 8,500 foot defiles, down steep gorges and across raging rapids in some of the world's most impenetrable jungles – stands as one of the greatest engineering feats of World War II. On 12 January 1945, the first official convoy pulled out of Ledo for Kunming over the newly finished Ledo Road. Commanded by General Pick, after almost a month of hard travel over the 1,100-mile route, the convoy rode triumphantly into Kunming. Before the war was over, more than 5,000 vehicles would make the trip, carrying 34,000 tons of vital supplies to China.[1]

After World War II, the Stillwell Road was virtually abandoned. No one in India thought of any link with Burma or China through this road. The portion from Pangsau Pass on the Patkai range leading to Myitkyina was neglected. Some time in the mid-nineteen fifties, a group of students from Cambridge University drove two Land Rovers from England to Shillong and then drove up the Patkai range, crossed the Pangsu Pass and drove along the Stillwell Road. They soon found the road ahead abandoned, the bridges overwhelmed with creepers and fallen. They managed to carry their two Land Rovers across the smaller streams taking the help of local villagers who ferried the vehicles across by slinging them on *bhaluka banh* (thick bamboos). When they reached the wider rivers and found the bridges fallen, they got the villagers to ferry the vehicles across on rafts. They managed to reach Mong Yu and then finally reached Rangoon and then Singapore. This pioneering expedition stirred little interest in India and the Stillwell Road was again forgotten.

Historical Background

It is of interest that the axis of the Stillwell Road was probably the same as the ancient southern silk route that linked China with Assam. The Ahoms who came to upper Assam in the early 13th century also probably followed the same axis. The Burmese Army that invaded Assam in the early 19th century also probably followed the same axis. The portion of the Stillwell Road from the Pangsu Pass to Myitkyina has since been improved to some degree by the Burmese government over the years. The road is in use from the Pangsu Pass on the Patkai range to Myitkyina a distance of 237 miles, passing through the following towns – Tawaga, Shijnpwinyan, Taronka, Daughnagar, Makaw, Tanai, Tinkok, Shartazyut, Wayazyut, and Mogaung. From Myitkyina to Bhamo it is116 miles and from Bhamo to Muse it is 90 miles. At Muse the Stillwell Road joins the Burma Road coming from Lashio and going to Kunming. The Chinese have developed the road from Kunming to Lashio and then on to Mandalay. Huge ten-wheeled trucks are regularly moving on this section.[2]

India's Failure of Foreign Policy on Burma.

From the time Burma got its independence, India had very good relations with the Government of U. Nu. The Burmese Army took over power in a silent coup in 1962, and finally in 1968, the Army Chief carried out another coup, and the military took full control of the country. In 1990, there was an uprising by the civil population against the military rule after the League for Democracy was not allowed to form the government after it won a clear majority of seats in the general elections held. In 1989, it is reported that the Burmese military sent a delegation to Delhi asking for help to build up their armed forces. At that time, the Indian Government probably read them a lecture on democracy. Rebuffed the Burmese delegation returned to Rangoon and opened negotiations with China. In China, the Communist party had recovered from the Cultural Revolution and Deng Hsiao Ping had reversed gears and embarked on a path of free enterprise. They had implemented a plan to develop the Kunming area and industrialise it to cater to the South and South East Asian market. The Chinese welcomed the Burmese delegation and supplied them with all their defence requirements of small arms, armoured vehicles, artillery, medium patrol boats. They also advanced soft loans of several billion dollars, with easy repayment facilities. The Chinese also developed the portion of the Stillwell Road that connected the Kunming area with Lashio and then to Mandalay. Very soon Chinese goods from the Kunming area were rolling down the Stillwell Road and flooding the Burmese market. From Mandalay the Burmese already had a road to Kalemyo, south of Tamu, the border town of Burma opposite Moreh. Soon Chinese goods were flooding the Indian market coming in through several channels, across Moreh in Manipur, from Nepal and entering India at Siliguri, and all along the Nepal border. The Government of India also considerately developed the Tamu Kalemyo Road. Along with the goods a sizeable Chinese population has also silently migrated to Burma. Mandalay has become a predominantly Chinese city. Our lack of foresight has cost us dearly. If we had helped the Burmese junta then, Burma would have been to a great degree dependent on us. The Stillwell Road should have been taken up for development then. But then, at that time, we were still in the Public Sector mode, while China with a communist government had already privatised.

China is importing raw materials from Myanmar and exporting readymade consumer goods to them. The Chinese town on the China Myanmar border – Rueli – is humming with activity. In 2006, 4.36 million people and 3,86,000 vehicles passed through Rueli's border crossing and carrying 4,75,000 metric tonnes of cargo. This includes, timber, gems, mineral and oil that go to China. Chinese consumer goods flood Myanmar's markets. Almost everything that Burma buys is from China and almost everything that she sells is to China. Thailand also buys raw material from Burma.[3] Chinese firms are by now involved in about 40 hydropwer projects and at least 17 on-shore and off-shore oil and gas projects in Burma. China has also announced plans to build a 2,400 km oil and gas pipeline from Arakan to Yunnan.[4] It is fairly obvious that China's grip on Burma is firm. The first reaction therefore, if the Burmese government permits development of the Stillwell Road to be taken up by India, will be a backlash of Chinese consumer goods from Rueli to Lashio, Myitkyina and then to the Pangsu Pass on the Patkai range and then into India. This will be for a simple reason that the route via Kalemyo to Moreh and Imphal will be too roundabout. When the Stillwell Road is opened, we cannot obviously prevent movement of goods from entering legally. We should not hesitate to open the Stillwell Road for this reason. We should see that Chinese consumer goods are beaten in competition by Indian goods. Incidentally, Chinese consumer goods are already in the Indian market, beating Indian goods in competition. Many Indian factories, of toys for example, have closed down because the Chinese toys are of better quality and cheaper, despite the long transportation.

Conclusion

What is likely to happen if the Stillwell Road is opened? The first development will be a sudden flush of Chinese consumer goods into India. This will probably cut down on smuggling from across the Manipur and Nepal borders. It will be good to encourage direct imports from China. This will stop the generation of black money that is a product of smuggling. It will also make the private sector in India strive to beat the Chinese in manufacture of consumer goods. Heroin is already being smuggled into India through Manipur, Arunachal Pradesh and Mizoram. It will now come along the Stillwell Road. Detecting and discouraging the smuggling of narcotics is the job of the border guarding force, the Narcotics Bureau and the Customs. The likelihood of more smuggling of narcotics along the new axis of the Stillwell Road should not deter us from opening the road. Opening of the Stillwell Road will benefit the economy of the people living on either axis of the road from the Pangsu Pass to Myitkyina. Civil supplies, medicines can be easier imported from India to cater for this region than supplied from Rangoon or Mandalay. The whole area will be opened up for tourism from India.

It is mentioned in this regard as to what is in it for Assam and the other North-Eastern states in opening this road. This is something that the North-Eastern states' industrial lobby, small as it is at present, should plan from now. A study should be made to list out what is being imported from China into Burma now. The lobby set up in Assam should then set up industries to manufacture such of those items that can undercut the Chinese supply. India can also import different kinds of gemstones and jade; also, timber and minerals.

Though the Government of India has been talking of a Look East Policy, this has not progressed beyond the idea expressed. Burma is presently in the throes of an internal agitation. After this settles down I think we should talk to the Burmese government and take up the opening of the Stillwell Road. The Border Roads Organisation developed the Tamu-Kalemyo, in 2000. They should be given the task of opening up the Stillwell Road and their flag should be flying on this route from the Pangsau Pass to Myitkyina and Lashio in near future.

Notes and References

1. Don Moser. *China-Burma-India.* World War Two. Time-Life Books.
2. "Stillwell Road in Historical Perspective", J.N. Phukan, *Reopening of the Stillwell Road – Prospects and Problems*. New Delhi, Anamika Publishers.
3. *Herald Tribune*, New York. 3 October, 2007
4. Myanmar and the World, *Economist*, 2007.

8
Connectivity and Economic Potential of Stilwell Road

Pradip Hazarika

Introduction

Why do we need to reopen the Stilwell Road?

Attempt is made here to address the issue from two important angles, viz. connectivity and economic potential. In other words, the case for reopening of the Stillwell Road will be argued from the point of view of (i) the possible contribution of the reopening of the road to improving connectivity of a whole landlocked region, and (ii) likely economic benefit it may open to the economies of the region. In fact, both these issues are complementary and interrelated and cannot be seen in isolation.

(A) Connectivity

The importance of connectivity from the point of view of

economic development needs hardly any emphasis. One of the major reasons for the relative economic backwardness of the North-East region of India is cited in its inaccessibility. The situation was however, very different at the point of Independence. Driven by expanding global trade and investment, the region was in the forefront of development, almost 150 years ago. Trade was conducted through the sea route, a network of inland waterways, and land transportation through road and railways. In fact, the railway network between Dibrugarh and Chittagong was one of the earliest projects in India implemented by the British in the late 19th century. The natural transportation route through East Bengal not only reduced the physical distance but also provided emotional closeness. Unfortunately, the partition of the country leading to the creation of East Pakistan changed the economic landscape of the region, virtually disconnecting it from the rest of the country. As a matter of consequence, today the North-East Region remains connected with the rest of the country by the chicken neck corridor of just 27 km at Siliguri. Further, today almost the entire boundary of the region (98%) is international border shared with Myanmar, China, Bhutan, Bangladesh, and Nepal. The partition of the country blocked the natural sea route through the port of Chittagong and landlocked the region and severed its market access and thus caused immense structural damage to the North-East economy. The NE Vision 2020 has therefore given topmost priority to strengthening the region's infrastructure and connectivity. In this connection the document has noted, 'Faster movement of goods and people at lower costs is essential to provide the impetus to economic activity. It helps the development of markets, reduces exploitation by middlemen, and in the process improves livelihoods of people in remote areas by enabling them to market their produce at higher prices.'

The re-opening of the Stilwell Road provides the easiest solution to the opening up of the economy of the North-East. If the Stilwell Road is reconstructed from Ledo in Assam to Myitkina in Myanmar, this road can then be extended to Moreh-Tamu (India) – Kalewa (Myanmar) crossing on the Chindwin river. The Indian engineers have already built this road – it was completed in 2001, and a bridge over the Chindwin can extend the road as far as Mandalay, which is on the Myanmar main railway system. Another North-Eastern state Mizoram, shares as much as 450 miles of border with Bangladesh and Myanmar, and if Bangladesh and Myanmar could be linked to Akyab (now called Sittwe) in Myanmar, and if Bangladesh agrees, Agartala could be connected to Chittagong. This will open up the entire North-Eastern region of India, making it the commercial outlet for the eastern trade.

(B) Economic Potential

The reopening of the Stilwell Road is likely to open up new-found opportunities, not known before, to the entire region. It would indeed not be out of place to mention that the Stilwell Road which formed part of the ancient southern silk route was used extensively during ancient times for travel and trade throughout the region and had immense economic, cultural, strategic and political significance. It was through this route that earlier, people of Burma, Assam (including those of the present Arunachal Pradesh viz. the Sinphos and Khamtis) and China, carried on their trade activities. It is further found from some early British records that out of several routes across the mountain ranges connecting North-East India with Myanmar, 'the Stillwell Road passing through the Pangsau Pass on the Patkai was the only one through which goods in bundle could be transported'. The route also remained facilitator and witness to many historic events which had shaped the culture and civilization of the entire area. One such event last immortalized is the migration of the Tai Ahoms under Chou-lung-Su-Ka-Pha. It needs hardly any mention that even today almost all inhabitants on both sides of the Pangsau Pass in India and Myanmar belong to the same racial stock and bear the same cultural traits. It is probably this affinity – both racial and cultural – which explains the continued informal, social and economic relationship among these people from both sides of the border, even after formal closing of the road after World War II.

The major potential economic gains from reopening of this important road can be explained in terms of three aspects:

1. Accelerated economic development to the North-Eastern states.

2. Expanded trade opportunities with South East Asian countries and China.

3. Significant new tourism opportunities.

a) Economic Development and Trade Opportunities

Trade has always been an important component of economic development. But connectivity is important for trade to flourish. I have briefly indicated how trade in the North-East flourished through the old trade routes. During the British period there were distortions to the traditional routes due to colonial decisions to 'draw hard lines between the hills and the plains, to put barriers to trade between Bhutan and Assam, and to treat Burma (Myanmar) as a strategic frontier as British India's buffer against French Indochina and China. However, the British provided the alternative connectivity by realigning trade through rail and road link, ultimately linking the same to ports at Chittagong. But post-colonial realignment of political boundaries once again distorted the entire scenario. To put it in the words of noted writer Sanjib Baruah, 'In post-colonial times, formally hard, albeit porous, international borders have worked against the North-East. The 'border effect' – tariffs and other market distorting effects of borders – has led producers to locate industries away from the region and closer to the core of the domestic market. Thus Barauni was supposed to be a better location than Guwahati for concentrating refining capacity.' When you suppress the natural course of action, the same will try other means. While on the whole, the trade economy shrank, informal border trade with neighbours flourished. A study by the Indian Institute of Foreign Trade (IIFT) way back in 1995, estimated the value of informal trade with Myanmar via Moreh alone at ₹ 2000 crores, which will be in current prices not less than ₹ 10,000 crores The same study estimated informal trade through Champhai in Mizoram at ₹ 500 crores and Lungwa in Nagaland at ₹ 100 crores. It is in view of the above that the Report of the High Level Commission on the North-East (S.P. Shukla Commission) emphasized the need to review the entire North-East border and inter-country trade issue, with particular reference to Bangladesh, Myanmar, South East Asia and South-west China. The report further recommended the creation of trade-related manufacturing possibilities in the North-East, required infrastructure and communication links, banking and warehousing facilities, necessary customs and security arrangements and manpower needs.

Look East Policy

Things have, however, moved on quite fast since the initiation of the Look East Policy, particularly on the foreign policy front, which has brought new hopes to the North-East Region. The first sea change on the policy front came in 1992, when the then Prime Minister P.V. Narasimha Rao launched the 'Look East Policy', in a significant shift in India's policy prioritization, with the objective of establishing closer economic integration with the South East Asian states and as concrete strategy to create an economic hub in its North-Eastern Region by exploring the trade and commerce potential with its ASEAN neighbours.

Delhi has already made significant efforts to open up North-East India to South East Asia. Almost 10 years back, the then External Affairs Minister Jaswant Singh on a visit to Myanmar, the first by an Indian Minister in 14 years, made a point that the natural outlet for India's North-East is through the neighbouring South East Asian countries and not Kolkata. "The North-Eastern states have to find an access eastward" – he told news reporters. Subsequently, India has built the Moreh-Tamu-Kalewa Road. Besides the Moreh-Tamu linkage, three new trade points were identified at Champhai-Rih, Pangsau Pass and Paletwa on the Kaladan river to enhance economic cooperation between the two countries.

Prime Minister Manmohan Singh referred to India's North-East as the gateway to the 'Asian Century' while inaugurating the Asian Car Rally, which was a successful Look East Policy event, at Guwahati, in November 2004. This policy holds the potential to make the North-East Region the commercial corridor of India linking the ASEAN nations, and enabling its people to harvest economic well-being through trade, transit and tourism.

In a written reply in the Rajya Sabha on 19 April, 2010, the Union Minister for Development of the North-Eastern Region (MDoNER), Shri B.K. Handique said that the Look East Policy was pursued in a multifaceted manner in diverse areas such as improved connectivity, promotion of trade and investment and cultural exchanges. Some of the important developments of the Look East Policy, relate to initiating/ resuming dialogue/trade with China, Bangladesh, Myanmar, Thailand and other countries of ASEAN.

Shri Handique said, the Look East Policy has also been pursued through constructive engagement with various regional groupings/organizations such as ASEAN, East Asia Summit, Bay of Bengal Initiative for Multi-Sectoral Technical and Economic Cooperation (BIMSTEC) and Mekong-Ganga Cooperation (MGC).

Some of the important developments under the above initiatives are as under:

India-ASEAN

- India signed a 'Trade in Goods' agreement with ASEAN in 2009, which became operational from 1 January, 2010.
- Negotiating FTA with Bay of Bengal Initiative for Multi-Sectoral Technical and Economic Cooperation (BIMSTEC)
- India's bilateral trade with ASEAN countries has grown from US$ 2.4 billion in 1990, to US$ 44.66 billion in 2008-09.
- So far, 7 Summit level meetings with ASEAN have been held.
- At the 7th ASEAN-India Summit, held in Thailand in October, 2009, among several initiatives to

strengthen economic cooperation with ASEAN countries, the trade target of US$ 70 billion within the next two years (by 2012) was announced.

East Asia Summit (EAS)

The concept of an East Asia Grouping was first promoted in 1991, by the then Malaysian Prime Minister. It provides India the forum to carve out for itself a larger East Asian strategic presence and taking forward our vision for the future. Thrust areas of the EAS include: (i) Energy, Environment, Climate Change and Sustainable Development, (ii) Education, (iii) Finance, (iv) Natural Disaster Mitigation, and (v) Avian Influenza. Four Summits of the EAS held so far.

Bay of Bengal Initiative for Multi-sectoral Technical and Economic Cooperation (BIMSTEC)

1. It has seven members – Bangladesh, Bhutan, India, Myanmar, Nepal, Sri Lanka and Thailand.
2. BIMSTEC provides a link between South Asia and South East Asia by way of economic cooperation and linkages in identified areas of cooperation.
3. Starting with 6 sectors, the BIMSTEC agenda of cooperation has expanded to 14 sectors: (i) Trade and investment, (ii) Technology, (iii) Energy, (iv) Transportation and Communication, (v) Tourism, (vi) Fisheries, (vii) Agriculture, (viii) Cultural Cooperation, (ix) Environment and Disaster

Management, (x) Public Health, (xi) People-to-people contact, (xii) Poverty Alleviation, (xiii) Counter-Terrorism and Transnational Crime, and (xiv) Climate Change.

Mekong Ganga Cooperation (MGC)

1. This brings together India and five ASEAN countries and was launched in 2000.

2. A vehicle for 'soft diplomacy' in countries that have had considerable cultural influence from India.
3. This has identified tourism, culture, education, and transport and communication as priority areas of cooperation.

Thus, the Government of India through initiatives under the Look East Policy is striving to attract optimum investments from the neighbouring countries to the North-Eastern Region, which will be visible in the long run.

The above positive developments will get a major boost if the Stilwell Road is reopened. Once the Stilwell Road is opened and the short stretch of unused road between Nampong in India and Mitikyina in Myanmar is reconstructed, the economy of the entire North-Eastern region will witness a sea change as the marketing zones of South China and South East Asia would be at a stone's throw distance. In such a situation, Assam will be directly linked with the Chinese business centre of Kunnming which is just

1079 miles (1,726 kms) away from Assam; much nearer in comparison to New Delhi and other major trading centres in India. With the opening of the new connectivity, business projects will open up not only with China but also with the other countries in South East Asia.

India spends huge amounts in transporting food items like pulses, poultry products, grains etc. to the North-East Region for which the people have to pay more to meet the cost of transportation. Likewise, prices of all other items that come from our hinterland are higher in the region reducing the affordability of its people. With better connectivity and the opening up of the trade routes with countries like Myanmar and Thailand – next door to North-East Region – can provide many of the items at much cheaper prices because of saving in the cost of carriage.

Better Trade Prospects with China and Myanmar

India China trade relations are the most important part of the emerging bilateral relations between India and China. From a temporary decline in the influx of Chinese imports in Indian markets, the scenario seems to have changed – India is enjoying a positive balance of trade with China. A recent study by the Federation of Indian Micro and Small & Medium Enterprises (FISME) has found that while trade in India and China is individually growing at 20-25 per cent a year, the growth rate of trade between the two countries is growing at a scorching pace, at double the rate of 50 per cent a year. With this level of growth, it is expected that the trade between the two countries would cross $100 billion mark by 2012. If one looks at India's imports from China, it is likely that Yunnan Province with its rich natural endowments may figure as the most important state of attraction. The principal exports from China to India include raw silk, beans, sheet and paper pulp, rosin, coke, medical products, light industry products, textile products, chemical industry products, food, metal products, machinery facilities, etc. The principal exports from India include iron ore sand, chrome ore, gem, steel, leather, plant oil, medicine, raw material for the chemical industry, etc. According to experts, one area which promises very quick growth in India-China trade is the import of Chinese silk yarn, especially the Yunnan variety, by India.

As regards Myanmar, it occupies a central place in India's Look East Policy. Myanmar is India's gateway to ASEAN as it is the only ASEAN country which has both land and maritime borders with India. With the Look East Policy in operation, India has emerged as the largest export market for Myanmar because it has the potential for meeting our ever-increasing need for items like pulses and beans. The most startling fact about bilateral trade between India and Myanmar is that it has grown more than eighty times in the last twenty eight years. From US$ 12.4 million in 1980-81, India-Myanmar trade grew steadily, to reach a level of 995 million US dollars in 2007-08. It went up still further after that. The actual trade turnover may probably be more if trade via third countries, particularly Singapore, and informal border trade is taken into account. The balance of trade is heavily in favour of Myanmar. Myanmar contributes to nearly one-fifth of India's imports of timber, second only to Malaysia, as timber and wood products accounted for nearly 30 per cent of Myanmar's exports to India. Myanmar is the second largest supplier of beans and pulses to India, next only to Australia.

b) Potential for Tourism

Tourism is another area which tends to flourish with the reopening of the Stilwell Road. With Look East Policy in place and a major boost to bilateral relations with the BIMSTEC and BICM countries in the last few years, resulting in a number of bilateral treaties on connectivity and other infrastructure projects, the atmosphere could not have been more ripe for going in a big way for cross-country tourism in India's North-East neighbourhood.

How can Tourism Improve?

Stilwell Road or no Stilwell Road, the objective environment for cross-country movement / travel for tourism purposes already exists:

- **Cultural and racial affinity**: India can always take advantage of the North-East's history and culture – the South East Asian roots of the Tai-Ahoms or the Khasis; Balinese Hinduism and art forms which are closer to Manipur. Further, in terms of topography, flora & fauna, food, dress habits, cultural beliefs and religion; there are so many things in common across the border, which would inspire people to travel from one side to the other and lead to cultural tourism.

- The tea gardens, oil fields, refineries, coal mines, forests, rivers etc. in adjoining areas of the Stilwell Road are likely to pave the way to development of business tourism.

- **Chance for educational tours:** Given the special characteristics of the area, there is much scope for anthropological and historical study, geological studies, studies based on bird watching, studies on butterfly, studies on reptiles, rain forests etc.

- **Stilwell Road itself is an object of tourist interest and attraction:** In view of its historical importance, everything that is special about the Stilwell Road can be a matter of attraction for a tourist, viz. the height and zigzag pattern which make the road adventurous and wonderful; the World War II cemetery and the 'Lake of No Return' on the course of the road, which immortalizes the Stilwell Road; the whole area through which the road passes, which is an area still unexplored.

The adjacent areas of Stilwell Road may provide scope for heritage tourism by way of having a taste of Tibetan culture in Arunachal Pradesh and the remnants of the Ahom Kings in Sivasagar, etc. There is also scope for festival tourism and pilgrim tourism if properly promoted.

Conclusion

The sub-region comprising North-East India, Bangladesh, Myanmar and South-west China, is a geographically contiguous area whose people interacted with each other through the Southern Silk Route from time immemorial. Much distortion had taken place to the trade, livelihood patterns and economy, due to disruption of this traditional route and the creation of artificial political barriers. Trade and exchange require connectivity – which has at present become limited and circuitous for the region which has invariably affected commodity and factor pricing, making the mode of production and distribution pattern less efficient and thus affecting the public welfare. There is thus a strong case for reopening of this historical route. Of late, under the Look East Policy of the Government of India, there has been a qualitative change in India's policy to our eastern neighbours and there has been a number of very positive steps in the area of bilateral cooperation leading to further improvement in connectivity, opening up and liberalization of border trades, collaboration in the field of exploration of natural resources, development of tourism etc. The atmosphere has thus become very ripe for removing the last straw in the reopening of the Stilwell Road. While the differences among political leaderships in the region have been drastically narrowed down and there is a genuine desire to come together for the common good, and there has been overwhelming support among the media, intelligentia, and above all, the common people in the entire region on both sides of the Stilwell Road. Let us wish that the reopening of this historic road will soon become a reality. So when there is so much urge and goodwill from the people and there has already been so much of the way forward, the dream of reopening Stilwell Road will possibly come true and it is only a matter of time now.

References

1. D., Nath, (ed.) *Reopening of the Stilwell Road: Prospects and Problems*; Kolkata, Maulana Abdul Kalam Azad Institute of Asian Studies, 2004, pp. 8-14.
2. Pradip, Hazarika, 'Stilwell Road: The Saga of Grit and the Swan Song of the Future', in D. Nath (ed.) 2004, *Reopening of the Stilwell Road: Prospects and Problems*, Kolkata, Maulana Abdul Kalam Azad Institute of Asian Studies.
3. "North-Eastern Region: Vision 2020", North-Eastern Council, Ministry of Development of the North-Eastern Region, Govt. of India, New Delhi.
4. Press release, "Ministry of Development of the North-Eastern Region," Govt. of India, New Delhi, April 20, 2010.
5. R.S., Mooshahary, 'India's Look East Policy Integrating the North-Eastern Region', 2005, Website: http://www.sicassam.in/contactus.html

PART II

9
Photo Essay on 'The Journey through the Stilwell Road'

Dilip Banerjee

The thirty photographs of this essay narrate the experience of Mr. Dilip Banerjee, the photo journalist, who along with two more scholars Mr. Phalguni Motilal and Miss Niharika Gupta had undertaken an arduous journey through the Stilwell Road in the year 2009. These photographs were taken by him during their month-long travel through this lost trail. The images have captured the nature, the people, the road, the trade and the day-to-day life of three nations, India, China and Myanmar, which were connected through this historical road. Instead of sequencing the photographs according to the road stress, they are kept at random, so that the cross-country culture and the economy can be visualised along with the existing scenario of the Stilwell Road. Dilip's photographs reveal a common chord of culture, economy, food habits and livelihood patterns of these three bordering regions of India, Southwest China and Northern Myanmar, and very vividly show their connectivity, similarity and interdependence. This journey through the Stilwell Road therefore not only brings out the changing infrastructure around this lost trail, but also explores, experiences and understands the emotional as well as economic linkages, which still exist amongst the people across the border. The photographs are the reflections of the truth of life, the oneness that is hard to deny, but which had painfully been disconnected by man-made borders and barriers. The captions of these photographs are given by Niharika Gupta.

The road going from Mu-se to Bhamo. Though exceptionally muddy, but travellers seem to be in good spirits.

An overview of the Lake 'No Return' from Pangsau Pass, which is surrounded by marshland.

The famous Jin Ma Bi Ji Fan Gate, where the first convoy of cars down the Stilwell Road entered on February 4, 1945. Nearby is The Hump situated, which is a bar, displaying World War II memorabilia that opened eight years ago.

Between the Indian and Myanmar checkpoints at the border.

The road leading north out of Myitkyina to Mogaung. Prior to the ceasefire, Kachin rebels would shoot from the hilltops.

The Stilwell Road is approaching Dali, the Southwest China. Dali is the centre of the Nan-chao kingdom from one of whose tribes the Myanmar settlers are descended.

A Bridge on the way back from Pangsau Pass.

A View in Kunming city, China.

Photo Essay on 'The Journey through the Stilwell Road'

Returning to Myitkyina by the Kamaing road from Lake Indawgyi.

Returning to Myitkyina by the Kamaing road from Lake Indawgyi.

A Bailey bridge on the route back from Pangsau Pass.

Zero milestone on the Stilwell Road.

A procession of novitiates near Mandalay, returning from the Sagaing Hill in the late afternoon, the girls, unsmiling in the heat, wear diadems of plastic flowers in their hair, their parents follow carrying the white cloth onto which their parents follow carrying the white cloth onto which their hair will be cut. They are on their way to the Mahamyamuni Pagoda and a nat shrine; for the next five days they are supposed to fast after lunch. To the rear of the procession are vans and a procession of horses. For men, the ceremony is to be undergone at least once in a lifetime.

Road widening was visible at many points on the road from Mu-se to Lashio.

Taking a left onto the Burma Road at noon, after three hours on the expressway, at Yunnanyi, on the way from Kunming to Dali. Yunnanyi also has an old airbase, with a mock-up of World War II fighter pilots. West of the road are fields and to the side of the road are small shops selling stationery, bulbs, spare parts.

Market-day, on the way from Tengchong to Lüxi. Items sold include dried spices, mobile phones, quilts, comic-books and textbooks, casseroles and electronic goods.

View of the Salween Bridge, which was rebuilt in the year 1955 from its guardhouse. Only the driver is allowed to cross with the vehicle, passengers are suppose to cross on foot.

At the border between the Kachin and Shan states, a new bridge over the Shweli river, with incense sticks placed at its base and what advertises itself as a "small store" nearby.

Approaching Ledo, Assam.

Gateway between China and Myanmar at the Ruili–Mu-se border. The image shows the Chinese side, where hotels, shops and jewelers are on a different scale from the buildings across the border, but crossing between the two worlds is an everyday affair for many Myanmar people.

The road to Bhamo, where motorable roads in many streches are almost non-existent.

Ledo Station, Assam. In the foreground are people from Andhra descended from those who left Burma during the War; many of these are working in Ledo's coal mines, and continue to retain cultural links with both Myanmar and with their extended families in Andhra Pradesh.

Salween Bridge, Myanmar.

Nearing Lashio.

A man is carried across the Wanding river for 500 kyat. Though this illegal passage takes up less time than the paperwork at border controls, if caught, onefaces a fine of 2000 yuan or imprisonment by the Myanmar government.

The bridge across the Shweli river.

Bridge at Wanri, where the road bifurcates towards the
One-Tree Forest and Moli, with a pipeline down the middle.
The bridge was constructedin the year 1961.

Cars are stuck deep in the mud near the gateway marking the entrance to the Kachin state.

En route to Bhamo, the forested hills near the China border are punctuated by the stray charred trees left by forest fires, the light lifting on banana leaves.

Profits through Border Trade: Myanmar girl counting out the rupees she has earned selling khow swe at Pangsau Pass.

Contributors

Prof. D Nath, Department of History, Dibrugarh University, Dibrugarh.

Prof. Lipi Ghosh, Department of South and Southeast Asia, University of Calcutta, Kolkata.

Shree D. S. Rajan, Director, Chennai Centre for China Studies, Chennai.

Ms. Soma Ghosha, Assistant Prof. S R S V M Kamarpukur, Hoogly.

Lt. General J. R Mukherjee, (Retired), Kolkata.

E. N. Rammohan, IPS (Retd.), Former Director General, Border Security Force, Assam, Government of India.

Pradip Hazarika, Member, Assam Legislative Assembly, Guwahati.

Dilip Banerjee, Photo Journalist, New Delhi

Index

Ahom documents, 3
Ahom king
  Siu-Ka-Pha, 3
  Sudangpha alias Bamuni Konwar, 35
  Suhungmung alias Dihingia Raja, 38
Ang, Chang, 31, 50
Aracan hills, 24
Arunachal Pradesh, 3–4, 13, 21, 56–57, 71–73, 88, 97–98, 102, 120, 126, 136
Asian Car Rally, 129
Asian Development Bank, 73, 98
Assam
  Ahom migration to, 48
  -Burma Route, 21, 39
  enjoys geo-strategic positioning, 103
  hazardous journey from Burma to, 50
Assamese chronicles, 3, 24–26, 30–31
Association of South East Asian Nations, 89
Ava Bridge, 5

Bangladesh-China-India-Myanmar Regional Economic Forum (BCIM), 80, 104
Barauni, 127
Bay of Bengal, 14, 63, 80, 103, 111, 130–131
Bay of Bengal Initiative for Multi-Sectoral Technical and Economic Cooperation (BIMSTEC), 80, 103, 130–132, 135
Better Trade Prospects with China and Myanmar, 133
Bhamo frontier, 24
Bhamo Road, 21
Bhaskaravarmana, King, 22
Border Roads Organisation, 83, 121
Bordoloi, Pradyut, 87
Brahmaputra Valley, 3–4, 26, 36–39, 47–48, 85
Buddhism, 37
Burma Road, 4, 6, 12, 28, 55, 86, 101, 115–117
Burma Star Association, 56, 102
China which won the anti-Japanese war, 52
China Youth Daily, 76
Chindwin River, 13, 111
Chinese consumer goods, 119–120
Chinese Theatre of Operations, 28
Churchills, Sir Winston, 115
Closure of borders, 2, 7
Colonial period, 45, 50, 84
Connectivity, 123–125
  importance of, 123
  movement of goods, 125
  peace and development, 90–91
Cross-cultural and trans-border movements, 2
Cultural Revolution, 118

Dalai Lama, 74–75
Dihing river, 30, 32
Drug routes, 93

East Asia Summit (EAS), 131
Economic and Social Commission for Asia and the Pacific (ESCAP), 104
Economic Potential, 125–136
  Economic Development and Trade Opportunities, 127–128
  Look East Policy, 128–129
  major potential economic gains, 126–127
Environmental Condition, 30–35
  bamboo rafts on the Dihing river, 30
  malaria-bearing mosquitoes, 34
  malarial terrain, 31
  Predominance of leech, 35
  profuse perspiration, 31
  thickly wooded jungle, 30
  topographic condition, 30
  tropical rain forests, 34

typhus-carrying mites, 34
Ephedrine, smuggling of, 93
Ethnic tension, 62, 104

Federation of Indian Micro and Small & Medium Enterprises (FISME), 133
Free trade zones, 93
French and British explorations, history of, 50

Global Times, 77
Golden Crescent, 96
Government of India Proposal, 57
Growth Triangle, 63

Himalayan-Patkai divide, 81
Historical Evidence, 22–24
Hiuen Tsang, 9, 22–23
Hydroelectric and hydrocarbon, 82

Importance of the Route, 35–39
  criss-crossing of people, 36
  human migration, 36
  political importance, 38
  regional trade, facilitate, 38
  rice culture, 37
  silk and silk industry, growth of, 37
India-China Relations, 67–75
  Agreement on Political Parameters, 72
  Arunachal Pradesh, claim, 71
  bilateral relation (2003) agreements, 69
  Bilateral trade, 69
  border talks, 69
  China-Pakistan nexus, 74–75
  Chinese intrusions, 72
  Chinese media rhetoric against India, 73
  'compromise-based' solution, 74
  confidence building measures (CBMs), 69
  congruence of interests, 68
  connectivity, growing, 70
  'finger point area' of Sikkim, 72
  foreign policy, 68
  geo-political transformation, 67
  growth in India-China trade, 134
  India-Dalai Lama relations, 75
  Manmohan Singh, visit to Arunachal Pradesh, 72
  McMahon Line, rejecting, 71
  Pratibha Patil visit to China, 70
  Promotion of Civil Nuclear Cooperation (2006), 69
  Rajiv Gandhi visit (1988), 68
  reforms, 68
  'Shared Vision for the 21st Century' (2008), 69
  'shelving' formula, 74
  1914 Simla Convention, 71
  Sino-Indian border talks, 71
  strategic interests, 67
  Tibet issue, 74
  win-win relationship, 68
Indian Chamber of Commerce, 97
Indian Institute of Foreign Trade (IIFT), 128
India's Failure of Foreign Policy on Burma, 118
Indo-ASEAN trade, 89
Indo-Myanmar
  Agreement (1994), 89
  border, 57, 81, 93–94
  Friendship Road, 83
  trade agreement, 83
  relations, improvement, 56
Insurgency, 12, 16, 53, 80, 91, 93–94, 96, 102, 104, 106, 108, 113
Inter-Asian linkages, 45
International highway-cum-trade route link, 57
Inter-regional cooperation, 64
Irrawady, 5, 23, 25

Khamjang-Nongyang Lake, 26
Khaplang, S.S., 94
Kuki National Army (KNA), 94
Kuki National Liberation Front (KNLF), 94
Kunming Initiative, 12, 63, 80, 86, 104
Kunming – Sitwe corridor, 111
Ledo-Bhamo-Dali Growth Triangle, 11, 61, 63
Ledo Road, 4, 21, 28–29, 34, 46, 55, 57, 87, 101, 116
Length of route, 6
Lifestyle and socio-economic conditions, 2
Local industries in Assam, 98
Look East Policy, 12–13, 15, 68, 80–82, 88, 91, 95, 102–103, 115, 121, 128–130, 132, 134–135, 137

Lung, Khun, 50

Man-a-Mile Road, 4
Mekong Ganga Cooperation (MGC), 80, 103, 130, 132
Mi mountain, 23
Missionaries, 4
Mong Mao Route, 3
Multi-lane international highway, 88
Multilateral cooperation, 96
Multilateral initiatives, 62, 95
Myitkyina-Patkai route, 3

Nambong, 32–33
Namjang Lake, 25
Nam Mao, river, 25
Nampong-Pangsau Pass, 56
Narcotics smuggling, 120–121
National Socialist Council of Nagaland, 94
NATO actions in Yugoslavia, 61
Neufville, Captain, 27
The New History of the Tang Dynasty, 47

Old Bisa Road, 21
Old Burma Road, 28
Old Opium Track, 5, 21
Oxford-Cambridge Overland Expedition, 53

Pangsau Pass, 3, 5, 21, 25–26, 28, 31, 35, 38–39, 56–57, 86, 93, 98, 101–102, 116, 121, 126, 129
Patkai range, 3, 9, 24, 27, 48, 53, 116–117, 120
Peaceful development goal, 11, 76
Peoples Liberation army (PLA), 77
Prophangpau (Puphangpom), 48

Qing dynasty period, 71

Railway system of Myanmar, 13, 111
Ramesh, Jairam, 88–89, 91
Reopening the road, advocacy, 88
Seagrave, Dr. Gordon, 34
Security concerns, 13, 106
Setong Sena, 88
Shan chronicles, 3, 24, 31–32
Shin Qamar region, 96
Silk Route, 2, 21, 137
Singh, Manmohan, 12, 72, 81, 83, 129
Sino-Indian dialogue, 61
Southern Silk Route, 21, 137
Special Accelerated Road Development Programme (SARDP), 97
Special Category Status, 108
Special Economic Zones, 64
S.P. Shukla Commission, 128
Stilwell, General Joseph, 6, 27–28, 39–40, 52–53, 101
String-of-pearls strategy, 76
Suspension of Operations (SOO), 94

Tai-Ahom Historical Passageway, 61
Tai-Ahom linkage, 48, 63
Tai-Shans, 48
Telecommunication linkages, 82
Tibet Autonomous Region, 74
Tourism, Potential for, 135–137
  cultural and racial affinity, 135
  educational tours, 136
  festival tourism, 137
  object of interest and attraction, 136
  pilgrim tourism, 137
Trade between ASEAN and India, 89
Trans Asian Highway, 61, 113
Trans-border transactions, 64
Trans-national trade partners, 103
Treaty of Yandaboo, 4
Treaty on the Patkai Pass, 40
Tripura-Bangladesh link, 14
Two-way trade and commerce, 2
United Liberation Front of Asom (ULFA), 59, 94
United National Liberation Front of Manipur (UNLF), 94

Vientiane Declaration, 80

Webster, Donovan, 4, 51, 56
World War II, 4–6, 21, 27, 30, 51, 53, 59, 86–87, 101, 116, 126, 136
Wu-ti, Chinese emperor, 24

Yi community, 92
Yunnan Province, 9, 29, 51, 57, 86, 91, 93, 134